حمن الرحيم

First published in 2003
Reprinted 2009
© Goodword Books 2009

Goodword Books
1, Nizamuddin West Market
New Delhi - 110 013
email: info@goodwordbooks.com
Printed in India

Abreviations used:
(saas - *sall-Allahu 'alyahi was sallam*)" May Allah bless him and
grant him peace (following a reference to
the Prophet Muhammad) (as - *'allayhi' s-salam*): Peace be
upon him (following a reference to the prophets or angels)

www.goodwordbooks.com

The Importance of Patience in the Quran

*Truly man is in loss—
except for those who believe and
do right actions, and urge each other
to the truth and to steadfastness.
(Surah Al-'Asr, 2-3)*

HARUN YAHYA

ABOUT THE AUTHOR

Now writing under the pen-name of HARUN YAHYA, he was born in Ankara in 1956. Having completed his primary and secondary education in Ankara, he studied arts at Istanbul's Mimar Sinan University and philosophy at Istanbul University. Since the 1980s, he has published many books on political, scientific, and faith-related issues. Harun Yahya is well-known as the author of important works disclosing the imposture of evolutionists, their invalid claims, and the dark liaisons between Darwinism and such bloody ideologies as fascism and communism.

His penname is a composite of the names *Harun* (Aaron) and *Yahya* (John), in memory of the two esteemed Prophets who fought against their people's lack of faith. The Prophet's seal on the his books' covers is symbolic and is linked to the their contents. It represents the Qur'an (the final scripture) and the Prophet Muhammad (peace be upon him), last of the prophets. Under the guidance of the Qur'an and the Sunnah (teachings of the Prophet), the author makes it his purpose to disprove each fundamental tenet of godless ideologies and to have the "last word," so as to completely silence the objections raised against religion. He uses the seal of the final Prophet, who attained ultimate wisdom and moral perfection, as a sign of his intention to offer the last word.

All of Harun Yahya's works share one single goal: to convey the Qur' an's message, encourage readers to consider basic faith-related issues such as Allah's Existence and Unity and the Hereafter; and to expose godless systems' feeble foundations and perverted ideologies.

Harun Yahya enjoys a wide readership in many countries, from India to America, England to Indonesia, Poland to Bosnia, and Spain to Brazil. Some of his books are available in English, French, German, Spanish, Italian, Portuguese, Urdu, Arabic, Albanian, Russian, Serbo-Croat (Bosnian), Polish, Malay, Uygur Turkish, and Indonesian.

Greatly appreciated all around the world, these works have been instrumental in many people recovering faith in Allah and gaining deeper insights into their faith. His books' wisdom and sincerity, together with a distinct style that's easy to understand, directly affect anyone who reads them. Those who seriously consider these books, can no longer advocate atheism or any other perverted ideology or materialistic philosophy, since these books are characterized by rapid effectiveness, definite results, and irrefutability. Even if they continue to do so, it will be only a sentimental insistence, since these books refute such ideologies from their very foundations. All contemporary movements of denial are now ideologically defeated, thanks to the books written by Harun Yahya.

This is no doubt a result of the Qur'an's wisdom and lucidity. The author modestly intends to serve as a means in humanity's search for Allah's right path. No material gain is sought in the publication of these works.

Those who encourage others to read these books, to open their minds and hearts and guide them to become more devoted servants of Allah, render an invaluable service.

Meanwhile, it would only be a waste of time and energy to propagate other books that create confusion in people's minds, lead them into ideological chaos, and that clearly have no strong and precise effects in removing the doubts in people's hearts, as also verified from previous experience. It is impossible for books devised to emphasize the author's literary power rather than the noble goal of saving people from loss of faith, to have such a great effect. Those who doubt this can readily see that the sole aim of Harun Yahya's books is to overcome disbelief and to disseminate the Qur'an's moral values. The success and impact of this service are manifested in the readers' conviction.

One point should be kept in mind: The main reason for the continuing cruelty, conflict, and other ordeals endured by the vast majority of people is the ideological prevalence of disbelief. This can be ended only with the ideological defeat of disbelief and by conveying the wonders of creation and Qur'anic morality so that people can live by it. Considering the state of the world today, leading into a downward spiral of violence, corruption and conflict, clearly this service must be provided speedily and effectively, or it may be too late.

In this effort, the books of Harun Yahya assume a leading role. By the will of Allah, these books will be a means through which people in the twentyfirst century will attain the peace, justice, and happiness promised in the Qur'an.

The works of the author include *The New Masonic Order, Judaism and Freemasonry, Global Freemasonry, Knight Templars, Islam Denounces Terrorism, Terrorism: The Ritual of the Devil, The Disasters Darwinism Brought to Humanity, Communism in Ambush, Fascism: The Bloody Ideology of Darwinism, The 'Secret Hand'in Bosnia, Behind the Scenes of The Holocaust, Behind the Scenes of Terrorism, Israel's Kurdish Card, The Oppression Policy of Communist China and Eastern Turkestan,Palestine, Solution: The Values of the Qur'an, The Winter of Islam and Its Expected Spring, Articles 1-2-3, A Weapon of Satan: Romanticism, Signs from the Chapter of the Cave to the Last Times, Signs of the Last Day, The Last Times and The Beast of the Earth, Truths 1-2, The Western World Turns to God, The Evolution Deceit, Precise Answers to Evolutionists, The Blunders of Evolutionists, Confessions of Evolutionists, The Qur'an Denies Darwinism, Perished Nations, For Men of Understanding, The Prophet Musa (as), The Prophet Yusuf (as), The Prophet Muhammad (saas), The Prophet Sulayman (as), The Golden Age, Allah's Artistry in Colour, Glory is Everywhere, The Importance of the Evidences of Creation, The Truth of the Life of This World, The Nightmare of Disbelief, Knowing the Truth, Eternity Has Already Begun, Timelessness and the Reality of Fate, Matter: Another Name for Illusion, The Little Man in the Tower, Islam and the Philosophy of Karma, The Dark Magic of Darwinism, The Religion of Darwinism, The Collapse of the Theory of Evolution in 20 Questions, Allah is Known Through Reason, The Qur'an Leads the Way to Science, The Real Origin of Life, Consciousness in the Cell, Technology Imitates Nature, A String of Miracles, The Creation of the Universe, Miracles of the*

Qur'an, The Design in Nature, Self-Sacrifice and Intelligent Behaviour Models in Animals, The End of Darwinism, Deep Thinking, Never Plead Ignorance, The Green Miracle: Photosynthesis, The Miracle in the Cell, The Miracle in the Eye, The Miracle in the Spider, The Miracle in the Gnat, The Miracle in the Ant, The Miracle of the Immune System, The Miracle of Creation in Plants, The Miracle in the Atom, The Miracle in the Honeybee, The Miracle of Seed, The Miracle of Hormone, The Miracle of the Termite, The Miracle of the Human Body, The Miracle of Man's Creation, The Miracle of Protein, The Miracle of Smell and Taste, The Miracle of Microworld, The Secrets of DNA.

The author's childrens books are: Wonders of Allah's Creation, The World of Animals, The Glory in the Heavens, Wonderful Creatures, Let's Learn Our Islam, The World of Our Little Friends: The Ants, Honeybees That Build Perfect Combs, Skillful Dam Builders: Beavers.

The author's other works on Quranic topics include: The Basic Concepts in the Qur'an, The Moral Values of the Qur'an, Quick Grasp of Faith 1-2-3, Ever Thought About the Truth?, Crude Understanding of Disbelief, Devoted to Allah, Abandoning the Society of Ignorance, The Real Home of Believers: Paradise, Knowledge of the Qur'an, Qur'an Index, Emigrating for the Cause of Allah, The Character of the Hypocrite in the Qur'an, The Secrets of the Hypocrite, The Names of Allah, Communicating the Message and Disputing in the Qur'an, Answers from the Qur'an, Death Resurrection Hell, The Struggle of the Messengers, The Avowed Enemy of Man: Satan, The Greatest Slander: Idolatry, The Religion of the Ignorant, The Arrogance of Satan, Prayer in the Qur'an, The Theory of Evolution, The Importance of Conscience in the Qur'an, The Day of Resurrection, Never Forget, Disregarded Judgements of the Qur'an, Human Characters in the Society of Ignorance, The Importance of Patience in the Qur'an, General Information from the Qur'an, The Mature Faith, Before You Regret, Our Messengers Say, The Mercy of Believers, The Fear of Allah, Jesus Will Return, Beauties Presented by the Qur'an for Life, A Bouquet of the Beauties of Allah 1-2-3-4, The Iniquity Called "Mockery," The Mystery of the Test, The True Wisdom According to the Qur'an, The Struggle with the Religion of Irreligion, The School of Yusuf, The Alliance of the Good, Slanders Spread Against Muslims Throughout History, The Importance of Following the Good Word, Why Do You Deceive Yourself?, Islam: The Religion of Ease, Enthusiasm and Excitement in the Qur'an, Seeing Good in Everything, How do the Unwise Interpret the Qur'an?, Some Secrets of the Qur'an, The Courage of Believers, Being Hopeful in the Qur'an, Justice and Tolerance in the Qur'an, Basic Tenets of Islam, Those Who do not Listen to the Qur'an, Taking the Qur'an as a Guide, A Lurking Threat: Heedlessness, Sincerity Described in the Qur'an.

CONTENTS

INTRODUCTION 10

THE QUR'ANIC DEFINITION OF PATIENCE...................12

THOSE WHO HAVE TRUE PATIENCE 15

THE PATIENCE OF THE FAITHFUL 18

WHEN THE FAITHFUL SHOW PATIENCE 29

THE BENEFITS OF PATIENCE................................55

THE SECRETS OF PATIENCE 65

THE PRAYERS OF THE FAITHFUL FOR PATIENCE 68

CONCLUSION..70

THE DECEPTION OF EVOLUTION 72

TO THE READER

* A special chapter is assigned to the collapse of the theory of evolution because this theory constitutes the basis of all anti-spiritual philosophies. Since Darwinism rejects the fact of creation—and therefore, Allah's Existence—over the last 140 years it has caused many people to abandon their faith or fall into doubt. It is therefore an imperative service, a very important duty to show everyone that this theory is a deception. Since some readers may find the chance to read only one of our book, we think it appropriate to devote a chapter to summarize this subject.

* All the author's books explain faith-related issues in light of Qur'anic verses, and invite readers to learn Allah's words and to live by them. All the subjects concerning Allah's verses are explained so as to leave no doubt or room for questions in the reader's mind. The books' sincere, plain, and fluent style ensure that everyone of every age and from every social group can easily understand them. Thanks to their effective, lucid narrative, they can be read at a one sitting. Even those who rigorously reject spirituality are influenced by the facts these books document and cannot refute the truthfulness of their contents.

* This and all the other books by the author can be read individually, or discussed in a group. Readers eager to profit from the books will find discussion very useful, letting them relate their reflections and experiences to one another.

* In addition, it will be a great service to Islam to contribute to the publication and reading of these books, written solely for the pleasure of Allah. The author's books are all extremely convincing. For this reason, to communicate true religion to others, one of the most effective methods is encouraging them to read these books.

* We hope the reader will look through the reviews of his other books at the back of this book. His rich source material on faith-related issues is very useful, and a pleasure to read.

* In these books, unlike some other books, you will not find the author's personal views, explanations based on dubious sources, styles that are unobservant of the respect and reverence due to sacred subjects, nor hopeless, pessimistic arguments that create doubts in the mind and deviations in the heart.

INTRODUCTION

O you who believe, be steadfast; be supreme in steadfastness... (Surah Al 'Imran, 200)

Allah has revealed in a verse, **"This is a Book We have sent down to you so that you can bring mankind from the darkness to the light, by the permission of their Lord, to the Path of the Almighty, the Praiseworthy"** (Surah Ibrahim, 1), thus drawing attention to the Qur'an's attribute of bringing people from darkness to light.

The Qur'an defines patience as one of the paths that lead people from darkness to light and as an attribute of morality that is superior to, wide-ranging, and very different from the daily behavior of many people. True patience is a moral characteristic displayed in the face of difficulty and in every moment of life. Moreover, it requires the demonstration of determination and consistency during times of ease and hardship, and is a lifelong endeavour that never goes astray, even for a moment.

Allah gives the most striking examples of patience in the lives of the Prophets, because they showed patience while teaching Allah's religion and leading a moral life. They never deviated from their devotion to Allah, and were patient people who sought only Allah's approval.

This book will define this high moral virtue taught by the Qur'an and invite people to acquire true patience. Inaccurate understandings of patience will be explained along with the kind of patience Allah requires, how Allah may test people so that they can acquire a more perfect patience, and the great return Allah promises to those who exhibit great patience.

Examples of how the Prophets showed patience in every area until the end of their lives will be presented in the hope that people will **"be steadfast for our Lord"** until the end of their own lives. (Surat al-Muddaththir, 7)

This book also will give the good news that Allah provided for those who respond to this call with the verse, **"give good news to the steadfast"** (Surat al-Baqara, 155). Moreover, emphasis will be placed on the facts that Allah is **"with the steadfast"** (Surat al-Baqara, 153) and that patience is a matchless key that opens doors to many fine things for the faithful. As Prophet Muhammad (saas) states:

Whoever remains patient, Allah will make him patient. Nobody can be given a blessing better and greater than patience. (Bukhari)

THE QUR'ANIC DEFINITION OF PATIENCE

O you who believe, seek help in steadfastness and prayer. Allah is with the steadfast. (Surat al-Baqara, 153)

Allah, Who has defined the best way of life for people and the most appropriate moral conduct for their nature, announces in **"We send down in the Qur'an that which is a healing and a mercy to the believers"** (Surat al-Isra', 82) that patience is a mercy for the faithful.

People can gain Allah's approval and love by fully applying the Qur'an's truths in their lives. Allah requires the faithful to adhere to the Qur'an's morality as long as they are alive, without showing any weakness. To carry out this task successfully, the faithful must acquire the supreme characteristic of patience, which is the result of faith. Those who learn the secret of patience can demonstrate the required steadfastness in every act and prayer.

Attaining this secret is extremely easy. Allah manifests His attribute "Al-Sabur" (The Patient) on those who believe in Him and helps perfect the determination in their hearts.

The real source of this lifelong true patience is the believers' faith in Allah. They know that Allah encompasses all things in His knowledge, that everything occurs only with His permission, and that He hides thousands of blessings and benefits behind all events.

In addition, they do not forget that Allah is the Friend, Guardian, and Helper of the faithful. Thus, although it may not seem so at first glance, all events are arranged to somehow benefit the believers. For this reason, patience is not a moral characteristic that makes life difficult for the faithful; rather, it is a form of worship that they accept wholeheartedly and with joy. Here is one point of difference between true patience and the view of patience as commonly understood in society.

Many people do not know the true meaning of patience, how truly patient people are required to behave, or how important this is in Allah's sight. They regard patience more as holding up one's head when faced with difficulties and problems, either overcoming or enduring them. Thus, they consider patience as the ability to withstand something, up to a certain point, and that an occasional loss of patience is quite normal. Moreover, according to this non-Qur'anic understanding, it is utterly futile to show patience in a matter from which no concrete benefit can be derived. And so when faced with such a situation, they give way to frustration and believe that being patient is useless.

The Qur'anic concept of true patience is quite different from this understanding of endurance. In the first place, people experience patience as the instruction of Allah and so can neither exhaust nor lose it. They carry out this form of worship joyfully and fervently and expect no concrete benefit in exchange for it, because they are patient solely to earn Allah's approval. What matters for them is the knowledge that they will earn His approval with their superior morality. For them, such a reward is enough.

Furthermore, the patience recommended by the Qur'an is not a moral characteristic employed only in times of hardship. True patience is shown in fully applying all of the Qur'an's teachings, in being scrupulous in guarding against all behavior that Allah warns against, and in being determined to live according to the Qur'an's morality as long as one is alive and with no thought of deviating from it, regardless of circumstances.

In **"But, in your Lord's sight, right actions that are lasting bring a better reward and are a better basis for hope"** (Surat al-Kahf, 46), Allah points out that proper behavior carried on with determination is regarded with approval and invites the faithful to be patient under all circumstances.

THOSE WHO HAVE TRUE PATIENCE

Therefore be patient with a beautiful patience. (Surat al-Ma'arij, 5)

Only the faithful understand the true nature of patience and live in the manner of which Allah approves, for they have accepted the Qur'an as their guide. And, only the Qur'an explains the real meaning of patience and the type of patience that is acceptable to Allah. For this reason, the only people capable of being **"patient with a beautiful patience"** are those who follow the Qur'an.

The source of their patience is their faith in Allah and their submission to Him. Like all of their other characteristics, patience emerges only through a true understanding of faith, because to believe is to understand that there is no deity but Allah, that He encompasses all things in His knowledge, that only Allah has the power to determine one's destiny, and that nobody can enjoy gain or suffer loss without His willing it.

One reason why the believers can show patience is because their faith enables them to appreciate Allah's might and glory. Those who know that Allah has boundless wisdom and boundless knowledge also know that only He can determine what will be the finest life for them. They know that Allah possesses all knowledge about all creatures and events in the past, present, and future, whereas people have only a limited intelligence that is prone to making mistakes in determining what is good and what is bad. In most cases, a seemingly unfavorable event may bring many benefits, although people may well be totally unaware of this. Allah points out this important truth: **"It may be that you hate something when it is good for you, and it may be that you love something when it is bad for you. Allah knows, and you do not know"** (Surat al-Baqara, 216).

Thus, knowing that only Allah possesses this knowledge and wisdom, the believers put their trust in Him, fully aware that whatever He wills is always beneficial, even though the benefit may not be immediately apparent. Therefore, they display true patience. In other words, one characteristic of those who have true patience is that they are people who have grasped and embraced the nature of destiny.

The Qur'an states that the faithful are patient and put their trust in Allah, as follows:

Those who are steadfast and put their trust in their Lord. (Surat an-Nahl: 42)

Another reason why the believers exhibit such a patient determination throughout their lives is their strong fear and consciousness of Allah. Just as they know that Allah has a boundless love and mercy for His servants, they also know that the punishment of Hell is eternal. Allah warns those who consider themselves too great to worship Him and who turn their faces away from Him of the torment to come. As the faithful are aware of this warning, they take pains to avoid it by being extremely careful and patient in implementing all of Allah's instructions and prohibitions. They channel their fear and consciousness of Allah into living the Qur'an's morality throughout their lives.

Awareness of this world's true face also ensures that the faithful will continue to be patient. As is stated in **"We will test you until We know those of you who strive hard [for the cause of Allah] and those who are steadfast, and test what is reported of you"** (Surah

Muhammad, 31), Allah makes a distinction between those who show patience in their worship of Him and those who manifest their resistance by becoming impatient. As a result, He will give those who worship Him in this life noble residences as hospitality in the next, while punishing those who deny Him with an eternal, inescapable Hell.

No matter what hardship they encounter, the faithful know that such hardship is a test from Allah and so do not lose their patience. How could they, knowing that they will face the Day of Judgment and receive their reward for their fine morality? Allah's Messenger (saas) also mentions that the believers remain patient when faced with calamity, since they always trust Allah, as follows:

The example of a believer is that of a fresh tender plant. From whatever direction the wind comes, it bends it. But when the wind becomes quiet, it becomes straight again. Similarly, a believer is afflicted with calamities (but remains patient until Allah removes the difficulty). (Bukhari)

One fundamental element of patience is exactly this—the believers have certainty about the Day of Judgment and the afterlife. Armed with the strength they derive from the knowledge that they will be tested here and rewarded on the Day of Judgment for every event for which they showed patience, and that Allah gives the good news of His mercy to those who show patience, they are committed to showing patience.

As we can see, only the faithful can experience true patience, because only they have bound and delivered themselves up to a sincere faith in Allah, have appreciated His might, and put their trust in destiny. In addition, they have a powerful fear and consciousness of Allah, have understood this world's true face, and believe firmly in the afterlife.

THE PATIENCE OF THE FAITHFUL

And be steadfast. Allah does not let the wage of good-doers go to waste. (Surah Hud, 115)

As we have seen, there are very significant differences between the believers' patience and that of a large section of society. The faithful regard patience as a method of drawing closer to Allah and live it as a form of worship ordered by the Qur'an. The Qur'an details this fine moral characteristic of the faithful, as follows:

Their patience is founded on trusting Allah

Most people show patience at times of severe misfortune when nothing else can be done. However, this type of patience has nothing to do with true patience. They can endure only when faced with misfortune, and do so only because they do not consider everything as a test from Allah, a test in which are concealed divine blessings or benefits. They make their spiritual state obvious by complaining about the problem and making various facial expressions. Until the situation ends, they cannot be rescued from their negative spiritual state.

The believers' true patience, however, is very different from mere endurance. They are aware that Allah creates whatever happens to them for a reason, and that therefore it contains some hidden benefit. Knowing that Allah has determined the best possible

The Patience Of The Faithful

destiny for them, they meet everything with pleasure and an open heart. Allah tells the faithful to adopt this attitude in the following verse: **"Those who are steadfast and put their trust in their Lord"** (Surat al-'Ankabut, 59).

No matter what the circumstances, the faithful do not complain or whine. In addition, Allah points out that His creation of difficulty together with ease is His immutable law: **"For truly with hardship comes ease; truly with hardship comes ease"** (Surat al-Inshirah, 5-6).

Allah reminds His servants of another important fact: **"Allah does not impose on any self any more than it can bear"** (Surat al-Baqara, 286). Allah tests everybody through the difficulties with which they can cope. Thus, if people experience problems, it is a certain truth that Allah has given them the strength to endure patiently.

Aware of such verses, the faithful do not regard patience as "suffering through a misfortune." They know that even if their troubles never end, these are concealed blessings and that the patient will be granted the finest returns in the afterlife. Thus, they are never overcome by troubles; rather, they pray to Allah to lighten their load in the knowledge that only Allah can overcome a problem, for He is the One Who sent it in the first place. They take refuge in Him and seek His help:

"Our Lord, do not take us to task if we forget or make a mistake. Our Lord, do not place on us a load like the one You placed on those before us. Our Lord, do not place on us a load that we have not the strength to bear. Pardon us, forgive us, and have mercy on us. You are our Master, so help us against the unbelievers." (Surat al-Baqara, 286)

Their patience is lasting

"But, in your Lord's sight, right actions that are lasting bring a better reward and are a better basis for hope." (Surat al-Kahf, 46)

People who practice the non-Qur'anic version of patience cannot experience patience as a continual and stable element of morality. One day they may show patience, but the next day they may show impatience.

But the faithful, who experience patience as an instruction of Allah and a requirement of their religion, never deviate from it. They strive to live their entire lives in a manner that pleases Allah and earns His approval as a result of their steadfast morality. Clearly, the behavior most pleasing to Allah is that of patience and steadfastness in all circumstances, because He tells us in the Qur'an that **"right actions that are lasting"** are more blessed.

In another verse, Allah gives the faithful the following instruction:

"Restrain yourself patiently with those who call on their Lord morning and evening, desiring His face." (Surat al-Kahf, 28)

Thus by conforming to this verse, the faithful display unceasing patience to earn Allah's approval.

They are patient for Allah's approval

Those who do not live by the Qur'anic morality hope that they will be rewarded for their temporary display of patience. When this does not happen, in their own words "their patience runs out," because they are patient only for worldly benefits. They forget about earning Allah's approval and that they will be held accountable for

The Patience Of The Faithful 21

their actions on the Day of Judgment. Allah informs His servants of this secret: **"Or did you imagine that you were going to enter the Garden without Allah knowing those among you who had struggled and knowing the steadfast?"** (Surah Al 'Imran, 142). Those who are patient in order to win Allah's approval will enter Paradise, whereas those who are patient only in hopes of worldly benefit will be deprived of this fine reward that Allah promises.

Believers, who are guided by the Qur'an and thus are aware of this fact, show patience only to earn Allah's approval. They expect no material reward. This attribute is stressed in one verse, as follows:

> **Those who are steadfast in seeking the face of their Lord. (Surat ar-Ra'd, 22)**

Their patience is joyful, willing, and wholehearted

The faithful display great patience when facing any difficulty, when carrying out fully the Qur'an's teachings, and by demonstrating the most steadfast morality under all circumstances. One reason why they can display this moral excellence at all times is because they understand that their most important task is to carry out Allah's commands. Thus they adhere joyfully and willingly to the Qur'an's morality. And, as a result, the knowledge that they will gain Allah's love, mercy, and assistance ensures that they will easily overcome any difficulty and will show patience at all times.

In one verse, Allah invites His servants to patience with the expression **"be patient for your Lord."** This ensures that they will adhere to His morality willingly no matter what may occur. Another reason for their display of wholehearted patience is that Allah informs us of His **"love of the patient"** (Surah Al 'Imran, 146).

Moreover, Allah has revealed **"Peace be upon you because of your steadfastness! How wonderful is the Ultimate Abode!"** (Surat ar-Ra'd, 24) to let the patient know that they will receive a fine reward on the Day of Judgment.

All of these blessings ensure that the faithful will live in patience with great joy and desire.

Their patience is never shaken

People whose fear and consciousness of Allah, as well as their faith in Him, are weak may modify their behavior according to other people or their surroundings or circumstances. They may behave well toward other people from whom they think they can benefit while displaying exactly the opposite behavior toward those whom they do not know or look down upon. For example, in societies that are far from religion, a shopkeeper who shows an exaggerated respect and interest toward a wealthy customer is a quite common sight. If such a customer causes difficulties or is capricious or condescending, the shopkeeper tolerates it all. But this same shopkeeper might not act as tolerantly when faced with even a justified request from a customer who might have only limited means. Moreover, such people who behave well toward others when life is good may change character completely when they are facing hardship. So long as a friend entertains them or provides them with opportunities, they behave very well. However, if that person falls on hard times and cannot help or entertain them as before, they may then become impatient.

This fickleness is due to their decision, conscious or otherwise, to build their moral values not upon the Qur'an's conception of morality but upon their own primitive understanding and benefits. In contrast, the faithful live out the Qur'an's morality, which is based on a fundamental faith solely to earn Allah's approval. Thus nothing in this world can cause them to lose their patience, which is one facet of their noble character. In contrast to other people, the faithful maintain their outstanding patience even in times of difficulty and hardship.

The Qur'an draws attention to this superior morality, as follows:

It is not devoutness to turn your faces to the East or to the West. Rather, those with true devoutness are those who believe in Allah and the Last Day, the Angels, the Book, and the Prophets; who, despite their love for it, give away their wealth to their relatives, orphans, the very poor, travellers, beggars, and to free slaves; and who establish prayer and pay alms; those who honour their contracts when they make them, and are steadfast in poverty and illness and in battle. Those are the people who are true. They are the people who guard against evil. (Surat al-Baqara, 177)

As this verse shows, Allah states that patience during hard times is a condition of true virtue. The faithful conform to this teaching and exhibit patience whenever they are confronted with hardship.

Their patience opens the way to superior morality

Since the faithful regard patience as a form of worship, their patience gives them several other fine characteristics, as follows:

The steadfast, the truthful, the obedient, the givers, and those who seek forgiveness before dawn. (Surah Al 'Imran, 17)

In another verse, Allah defines the faithful as **"Those who give in times of both ease and hardship, those who control their rage and pardon other people"** (Surah Al 'Imran, 134). All of these characteristics can be experienced only through a heartfelt acceptance of the Qur'anic concept of true patience.

Overcoming anger and remaining calm over a long period of time is possible only by exercising patience. Those who help people even when they themselves are experiencing hardship can do so only because they are patient for the sake of Allah. They behave this way because they know that helping others at such times will help them earn Allah's approval. The ability of a just person to pardon an unjust one also is a characteristic of true patience.

In the same way, lifelong obedience to Allah's commands and prohibitions is possible only through patience. The faithful display decisiveness in self-sacrifice, goodwill, modesty, forgiveness, honesty, loyalty, and affection, and live out these moral characteristics through patience.

As we have seen, patience opens the road for the faithful to a superior morality of which Allah approves. For the faithful, living this morality earns His endless blessing and a place in Paradise. There can be no finer salvation.

Their patience is an intelligent patience

It would be a serious mistake to think that the believers' patience is only a matter of waiting to remove obstacles and overcome difficulties without making any effort. On the contrary, Allah instructs them to make every effort to secure the people's tranquility and comfort by making full use of their minds, consciences, and opportunities. For this reason, they maintain a heartfelt patience in the face of troubles, and yet strive with all their might to remove the source(s) of the problem.

For example, finishing an urgent task may give rise to incorrect behavior in impatient people. In particular, many people become very angry at the prospect of losing a large expected profit through human error, for they do not consider the possibility that this could be a hidden blessing. Believers, in contrast, trust Allah no matter how great the loss may be, and continue to be serene and at ease. However, they also take all of the precautions they can to prevent this from happening again. They warn the person(s) who made the mistake, turn it over to a more qualified person, or take even more precautions.

People who are unaware of the Qur'an's concept of patience regard patience as a matter of simply waiting without making any effort. In fact, they consider such helpless behavior as extremely virtuous. Allah, in contrast, encourages people to overcome their difficulties by exhibiting patience and using their minds, consciences, and material resources. Several verses draw our attention to such facts, such as in the case of those who migrated from Makka to Madina, as follows:

But to those who emigrated after they were persecuted and then strove and remained steadfast, to them your Lord is All-Compassionate, Most Merciful. (Surat an-Nahl, 110)

In addition to this, while taking active measures in the face of difficulties, believers also continue to pray to Allah for assistance, for this is what the Qur'an tells them to do, as follows:

When they came out against Talut and his troops, they said:

"Our Lord, pour down steadfastness upon us, make our feet firm, and help us against this unbelieving people." (Surat al-Baqara, 250)

As can be seen, the patience of the faithful is an intelligent patience. Such behavior will receive the finest reward in Allah's presence.

In patience, the faithful know no limits and compete with one another

As stated in **"No indeed! Truly man is unbridled, seeing himself as self-sufficient"** (Surat al-'Alaq, 6-7), the faithful know that regarding themselves as competent in any field leads to excess and conceit. Thus they do not consider themselves competent even if they perform some tasks perfectly. Throughout their lives, they strive to develop themselves and achieve a finer, better behavior.

Behind these sincere efforts lies their attachment to and love of our Lord, and their fear and consciousness of Him. Since their greatest aim is to achieve His love and approval, they try to live according to the spirit and the letter of the Qur'an's teachings. Aware that they can never be adequate in such a task, they always strive to put even more effort into adhering to His teachings in this life.

They know that the amount of effort they make will earn a commensurate reward in Allah's presence and that, to this extent, they can easily be united with His blessings. With the words, **"Race each other to forgiveness from your Lord and a Garden [i.e., Paradise] as wide as the heavens and the Earth, prepared for the people who guard against evil."** (Surah Al 'Imran, 133), Allah urges the faithful to compete in good with each other in order to gain His approval and a place in Paradise. One of these matters is patience, as we read: **"O you who believe, be steadfast; be supreme in steadfastness"** (Surah Al 'Imran, 200). In such cases, the faithful know that they will earn Allah's love and closeness to Him, and so compete with one another to display their best behavior. The believers are patient regardless of their circumstances and, trusting in our Lord, show their determination through their consistent behavior. Even when confronted with totally unexpected developments, such as being forced to live in the streets or a shelter because their houses have burned down, they do not complain or think "if only it had not happened." They understand that Allah has sent a hidden blessing to them, and so live in the tranquility that this understanding brings. They continue this behavior even if faced with another event that makes their situation even worse. In short, no matter what terrible difficulties they may face, they race each other to patience, as Allah has ordered.

They encourage one another to be patient

In the verse: **"Let there be a community among you who call to the good, and enjoin the right, and forbid the wrong. They are the ones who have success"** (Surah Al 'Imran: 104), Allah instructs the faithful to divert one another from evil by advising what is good and guiding one another toward positive behavior. In line with this, the faithful spend their lives calling upon one another to follow the Qur'an in full and to avoid all that Allah has forbidden. In particular, they encourage patience, because they know that those who adhere to the morality that Allah loves will reach Paradise, while others will be condemned to the torment of Hell. Therefore, they want all who are faithful to earn the right to enter Paradise as much as they desire their own salvation. For this reason, they call on the faithful to be patient in all their acts of worship and while going about their daily lives. The Qur'an gives the example of this when our Prophet (saas) and his companion were in the cave on their way to Madina:

If you do not help him, Allah helped him when the unbelievers drove him out and there were two of them in the cave. He said to his companion, "Do not be despondent, for Allah is with us." Then Allah sent down His serenity upon him. (Surat at-Tawba, 40)

Even while hiding under extremely difficult conditions from people who might have killed him, the Prophet (saas) reminded his companion of Allah's assistance. All Muslims should learn from and follow this example. Guiding one another toward patience by mentioning the strength and assistance of Allah whatever the circumstances may be indicates superior morality.

The Qur'an refers to such people as "**the Companions of the Right**":

[Have We not] shown him the two highways? But he has not braved the steep ascent. What will convey to you what the steep ascent is? It is freeing a slave or feeding on a day of hunger, an orphaned relative or a poor man in the dust; then to be one of those who believes and urge each other to steadfastness and compassion. Those are the Companions of the Right. (Surat al-Balad, 10-18)

WHEN THE FAITHFUL SHOW PATIENCE

Except for those who are steadfast and do right actions. They will receive forgiveness and a large reward. (Surah Hud, 11)

So far, we have described the Qur'anic understanding of patience and have highlighted how it differs from the understanding held by those who are far from religion. In this section, we will explain what believers are patient with by comparing their behavior with the impatience of the unbelievers.

However, before going into detail on this matter, we should be aware of the fact that Allah tests His servants by sending troubles to them at a time of His choosing. This may be a momentary or a long-term test, but one thing is certain: In the afterlife, regardless of what they faced while in this world, the finest life is the one lived by those who are faithful to Allah. Allah announces this in the following verse:

Anyone who acts rightly, male or female, being a believer, We will give them a good life and recompense them according to the best of what they did. (Surat an-Nahl, 97)

The faithful are patient when Allah tests them and, as a result, receive His help in their effort to overcome these problems. He eases the believers' tasks and helps them, as follows:

Allah will certainly help those who help Him—Allah is All-Strong, Almighty. (Surat al-Hajj, 40)

Following their consciences

In the coming pages, we will analyze the principal circumstances during which the faithful, with Allah's support, exhibit patience.

Allah created each person with a conscience to let him or her know what is right and wrong in all situations. This conscience calls upon people to think in the manner that pleases Allah and behave in the manner that will earn His approval. Every person also has a lower self that urges them to follow their whims and desires. However, believers always display a sure determination to ignore their lower selves by listening only to their consciences, even if their lower self calls them to something that appears more attractive and more appealing.

Throughout their lives, the faithful make this judgment call and then select the most correct attitude. In daily life, this can mean ignoring the lower self's urging to behave selfishly by following the conscience's advice to be self-sacrificing. In the case of finishing an important task or when faced with many things at the same time, it may require a person to assist somebody who needs even more help at that specific time. Or it may require the faithful to share something that they need with someone who needs it even more, or even to give it to that person. Those who obey their conscience exhibits good behavior without hesitation. In other words, they do whatever they can to help others who need assistance. The Qur'an gives an example of this morality, as follows:

> **Those who were already settled in the abode and in faith, before they came, love those who emigrated to them. They do not find in their hearts any need for what they have been given, and prefer them [the emigrants] to themselves, even if they**

themselves are needy. Those people who are safe-guarded from the avarice of their own selves are successful. (Surat al-Hashr, 9)

This behavior of the faithful, as depicted in the Qur'an, is the result of the extreme patience they display while following their consciences.

Ignoring Satan's wiles

When Allah created Prophet Adam (as), He required all angels to prostrate to him. However, Iblis rebelled against Allah's order and refused to do so.

Faced with Satan's rebellion, Allah cast him out of Paradise and declared him cursed until the end of time. But Satan demanded that Allah allow him to tempt people to loose themselves in the allures of this world until the Day of Judgment, when they would be resurrected. Allah granted this, but also declared that Satan would have no power over His faithful servants:

He [Satan] said: "My Lord, because You misled me, I will make things on Earth seem good to them, and I will mislead them all, every one of them, except those of Your servants among them who are sincere." He [Allah] said: "This is a Straight Path to Me. You have no authority over any of My servants, except for the misguided who follow you." (Surat al-Hijr, 39-42)

As can be seen, after Adam (as) was created, Satan began working to tempt people to stray from Allah's path. Thus, the faithful are responsible for showing patience by their continual awareness of the traps that Satan sets for them and their refusal to yield to his whispering.

Satan approaches all people with a variety of illusions and deceits. People may encounter his plots quite often in their daily lives, for

Satan meets them in unexpected places. He provides them with false hopes and fears, all of which are designed to lead people into heedlessness, idleness, and postponing good works. For example, those who are trying to help the poor for Allah's approval may face such suggestions as: "If you spend what you have, later on you will have problems." Or, Satan may try to make people forget a task that will benefit Islam and the Muslims. However, they must not forget that "**Satan's scheming is always feeble.**" (Surat an-Nisa', 76).

Satan cannot influence those who display patience in maintaining their faith in our Lord, because Allah has declared that Satan can deceive and divert only those who rebel against Allah, as he himself did. In **"If an evil impulse from Satan provokes you, seek refuge in Allah. He is All-Hearing, All-Seeing"** (Surat al-A'raf, 200), Allah calls on the faithful to take refuge in Him from Satan's wiles and deceptions.

The faithful who follow this advice spend their lives fighting Satan's games and tricks, for they understand that just as Satan's whispering is a full-time job designed to lead people to Hell, it is their full-time job to resist his whispering. If they feel any hesitation or slackness about doing something that will bring good, they take refuge in Allah and concentrate on the task with great enthusiasm. Such an understanding is mentioned in the following verse:

> **As for those who believe, when they are bothered by visitors from Satan, they remember and immediately see clearly. (Surat al-A'raf, 201)**

Heeding Allah's advice, **"O you who believe, seek help in steadfastness and prayer. Allah is with the steadfast"** (Surat al-Baqara, 153), in order to guard themselves against Satan, they ask for our Lord's help and set their faces against Satan's deceptions, saying:

Say: "My Lord, I seek refuge with You from the goadings of the devils, and I seek refuge with You, my Lord, from their presence." (Surat al-Mu'minun, 97-98)

Unceasing adherence to a steadfast morality

Allah has placed upon everybody the responsibility for heeding the Qur'an and living out its superior morality. Thus, on the Day of Judgment people will be asked if they have followed the Qur'an's morality or not. Everyone who has ever lived, and who will ever live, has been advised of this truth and invited to conform to the morality that pleases Allah. But the only people who heed this call are those who have faith.

In those communities that are far from religion, some people may live out certain aspects of the Qur'an's morality, such as being self-sacrificing, kindhearted, merciful, just, and benevolent. But no matter how moral they claim to be, there will be moments when they display impatience. For example, a person may be late for an important business meeting for a variety of reasons, and then get caught in a traffic jam while trying to reach the meeting place. He might not be able to call his office in time to let them know that he will be late, and he might have missed the meeting by the time he finally arrives. Thus he might respond angrily or just glare and remain silent if someone else asks him a question at that very time. Even though the person in question might consider himself helpful and understanding, in such circumstances he shows that this is not the case all the time by saying that "his patience has run out."

People who do not live the Qur'an's morality are often plunged into unnecessary anger when confronted with certain events. For example, a secretary may forget to send a very important message, a child may break the most valuable object in the house, a wife may have an accident with the car that her husband has been making payments on for years, or a relative may visit at an inconvenient time, and so on. These are common occurrences, and those who do not display the Qur'an's morality might slip into rather unpleasant behavior. The reason for such behavior is their inability to show patience in living by the values that Allah prescribed.

Only those who possess the superior morality portrayed in the Qur'an can always display true patience. Their most important characteristic is the unchanging nature of their behavior. For example, one might have a very strong temper, but upon learning that Allah refers to believers as **"those who control their rage and pardon other people"** (Surah Al 'Imran, 134), he or she exhibits forgiving behavior even when faced with an event that normally might cause them to become angry. Whatever may happen, believers continue to speak pleasantly, remain tolerant, control their anger, and show other fine moral characteristics taught by the Qur'an.

In short, what makes the believers' character superior is their consistency and patience at all times, both of which enable them to live by their high morality. The faithful try to display consistency as long as they are alive not only in pardoning other people but also in displaying self-sacrifice, humility, compassion, kindheartedness, tolerance, justice, love, and respect, and by exercising their free will, because Allah tells the faithful to be consistent in their worship: **"He is Lord of the heavens and Earth and everything in between them, so worship Him and persevere in His worship"** (Surah Maryam, 65).

Another command of Allah is to answer evil with good. The Qur'an tells the faithful to distance themselves from evil as best they can by remaining patient, as follows:

A good action and a bad action are not the same. Repel the bad

with something better and, if there is enmity between you and someone else, he will be like a bosom friend. None will obtain it but those who are truly steadfast. None will obtain it but those who have great good fortune. (Surah Fussilat, 34-35)

As a result of this patience and determination shown by the faithful, Allah gives them the finest reward for what they have done, and allows them to enter Paradise. He gives this news in the following verse:

What is with you runs out, but what is with Allah goes on forever. Those who were steadfast will be recompensed according to the best of what they did. (Surat an-Nahl, 96)

Fearing nothing but Allah

People who have not grasped Allah's power and greatness are vulnerable to innumerable fears, among them the fear of other people, the dark, or certain numbers or colors, believing that they have an independent power of their own.

Meanwhile, the faithful know that only Allah has power and that nobody can harm or help anybody else without His permission. They are aware of the fact that no people or creatures can have power that is independent of Allah, and that everything owes its existence to Him. If they encounter some harm, they believe wholeheartedly that only our Lord can remove it. Allah tells the faithful to fear nothing but Him, as follows:

It was only Satan frightening you through his friends. But do not fear them—fear Me, if you are believers. (Surah Al 'Imran, 175)

Due to their firm belief and trust in Him, the faithful experience no sadness or depression when confronted with frightening or intimidating events. Oppression or limitations do not cause them to swerve in their devotion to Him and their striving to earn His approval. The Qur'an explains this attribute, as follows:

Those to whom people said: "The people have gathered against you, so fear them." But that merely increased their faith, and they said: "Allah is enough for us, and [He is] the Best of Guardians." (Surah Al 'Imran, 173)

As this verse indicates, even if the faithful are faced with pressure, they fear only Allah and show their patience by not abandoning their faith. Allah has declared that He will test His servants with fear to separate the true believers from those who have weak—or no—faith. In exchange for this, He gives the following good news to those who remain patient in their faith:

We will test you with a certain amount of fear and hunger and the loss of wealth, life, and fruits. But give good news to the steadfast. (Surat al-Baqara, 155)

When faced with property damage

Allah has decorated the life of this world with many beautiful things and has created an environment from which people can derive pleasure. They are required to use the blessings showered on them in the best possible way, without becoming passionately attached to them. They realize that whatever people acquire here will remain here, and that they will have to account for their use of these blessings in our Lord's presence on the Day of Judgment. Those who understand that everything is a gift from Allah and show gratitude to Him will be rewarded, while those who forget the Day of Judgment, and so try to seize these blessings for themselves with greed, will suffer disappointment.

In the Qur'an, Allah lists some of the many blessings that He has granted to people, as follows:

To mankind, the love of worldly appetites is painted in glowing colors: women and children, heaped-up mounds of gold and silver, horses with fine markings, and livestock and fertile farmland. All that is merely the enjoyment of the life of this world. The best homecoming is in the presence of Allah. (Surah Al 'Imran, 14)

The faithful use these blessings in the best possible way, but at no time become addicted to them. They know that, as with everything else in the world, possessions and goods are part of the environment created to test them. Knowing that the blessings of this world are transient and that the home of the real blessings, none of which will ever be lost, is the afterlife, they have no worldly ambitions.

Since they feel neither ambition nor passion for worldly goods, they show patience whether times are good or bad. When they lose their property or it is damaged, they do not sink into sorrow or worry. If they obtain a large amount of property by working for years and then lose it all in a day, they know that Allah is testing their faith and patience. Therefore, they do not become distraught if their houses, orchards, or gardens are destroyed, or if their businesses end up going bankrupt. Despite all of these trials, they live in the comfort provided by the knowledge that Allah will ease their burdens, clear their way, conclude matters to their benefit, and reward their patience with better things in the afterlife.

People who are passionately attached to this life cannot stand it when their hard-earned property suffers any loss or damage, and so display rebellious behavior. Forgetting that Allah is the true owner of all property and that He can give more than He has taken away, if He so wills, they cannot see any good in such an event and so cannot show any patience.

As Allah tells us in "**We will test you loss of wealth and life**" (Surah Al 'Imran: 186), such tests reveal the difference between the faithful who show patience for the sake of Allah and those who pursue property and forget about the afterlife. The faithful do not grieve when they lose their property, for their only intention is to use everything they possess physically and spiritually to earn Allah's approval. In other words, they have already devoted these possessions to Allah. In return for their devotion, they receive the following reward:

Allah has bought from the believers their selves and their wealth in return for the Garden ...

... Rejoice, then, in the bargain you have made. That is the great victory. (Surat at-Tawba, 111)

Facing hunger or poverty

In addition to testing people with fear, a loss of property or their business, or illness and other things, Allah may also test them with poverty and hunger.

However, it should be realized that Allah creates a different test for every person. For this reason, not everyone will face all of these tests in the same way and under the same conditions. In fact, Allah creates the secret of the test by sending the same test to people in a wide variety of forms and in unexpected ways. Those who have true faith and devotion are prepared to face these difficulties in all of their forms by relying on the power of their faith and their submission to Allah.

In such situations, the unbelievers' behavior is far from resignation. They forget that only Allah gives the countless blessings that they encounter in this world, and so they show Him no gratitude. In fact, if even one blessing is removed, they rebel against Allah and show ingratitude. In communities that are far from religion, one can find such examples on a regular basis. Rich people who become poor lose many blessings that Allah has bestowed upon them in the past. Ignoring the fact that their houses, cars, clothes, foods, and drinks were Allah's gifts to them, they believe that all such things belonged to them alone. Unable to learn the intended lesson and ask Allah to grant new blessings, they do not put their trust in Allah and thus turn a beneficial test against themselves.

On the other hand, those who are aware of these truths and show steadfast patience, who remain pleased with our Lord when rich or poor, hungry or fed, will be rewarded with Allah's mercy. Allah proclaims the good news that those faithful people who are grateful to Him will have their blessings increased: **"And when your Lord announced: 'If you are grateful, I will certainly give you increase. But if you are ungrateful, My punishment is severe'"** (Surah Ibrahim, 7).

The Qur'an also informs the faithful who are tested by hunger and poverty, as follows:

Or did you suppose that you would enter Paradise without facing the same as those who came before you? Poverty and illness afflicted them, and they were shaken to the point that the Messenger and those who believed with him said: "When is Allah's help coming?" Be assured that Allah's help is very near. (Surat al-Baqara, 214)

Allah tells us that these people were afflicted with poverty and illness and sought refuge in His help. We must always remember that He gives the good news that for those who are patient and meet such a test with good behavior, whatever the circumstances, His help is very near at hand. We know this because He promises that while testing the faithful, He will ease their burden. This situation, as proclaimed in "**For truly with hardship comes ease**" (Surat al-Inshirah, 5), ensures that the faithful are pleased with what Allah has given, and that they will continue to show patience even in their darkest hours.

In the following hadith, our Prophet (saas) advises believers to be patient and trust Allah:

"Be mindful of Allah, [for] you will find Him before you. Get to know Allah in prosperity, and He will know you in adversity. Know that what has passed you by was not going to befall you, and that what has befallen you was not going to pass you by. And know that victory comes with patience, relief with affliction, and ease with hardship." (Tirmidhi)

We can see some of the finest examples of such behavior among the Prophet's (saas) Companions. In order to win Allah's approval, they remained patient on His path despite thirst, poverty, and intolerable hunger, and continued to struggle along with our Prophet (saas). Allah mentions the reward that they would receive in exchange for their superior morality, which they displayed by remaining patient in the face of exhaustion, as well as the hunger and thirst they experienced in their sweltering desert surroundings, as follows:

It was not for people of Madina, and the desert Arabs around them, to remain behind the Messenger of Allah or to prefer themselves to him. That is because no thirst or weariness or hunger will afflict them in the Way of Allah, nor will they take a single step to infuriate the unbelievers, nor to secure any gain from the enemy, without a right action being written down for them because of it. Allah does not let the wage of the good-doers

go to waste. (Surat at-Tawba, 120)

As we can see, Allah announces that the patience displayed by the faithful who are being tested will be rewarded, and that none of their good acts will be overlooked, on the Day of Judgment. He also proclaims His mercy toward the faithful by describing them as those **"who [He] has preserved them from hunger and secured them from fear" (Surah Quraysh, 4).**

When struck with illness

In societies characterized by the lack of Qur'anic morality, it is considered quite normal that people's behavior will change according to circumstances. They will exhibit good behavior when they can meet all of their physical and spiritual needs easily and ensure their own comfort, but will change completely when faced with any problem that may endanger their comfort. They cannot meet even a temporary affliction with patience. This becomes very clear in the case of illness.

How people behave during times of illness, hunger, exhaustion, and similar events are clear indications as to whether they do—or do not—possess sound morality. Given this fact, difficult times are very valuable opportunities for people to prove their faith in, devotion to, and trust in our Lord. Allah states that among the conditions for true morality and true goodness is showing correct behavior by being patient in times of trouble and sickness (Surat al-Baqara, 177).

When faced with such a problem as illness, what enables the faithful to behave steadfastly and with patience is their deep attachment to and faith in Allah. Prophet Ibrahim (as) expressed this truth by saying **"and when I am ill, He heals me"** (Surat ash-Shu'ara': 80).

Like Prophet Ibrahim (as), believers also know that Allah creates both the illness and the cure, and so they are not seized with despair when they fall ill. On the contrary, they are grateful to our Lord for those years in which He allowed them to live in health. Understanding that a healthy life is only one of Allah's many gifts to them, they continue to behave gratefully even when they are ill.

They also continue to be extremely grateful and steadfast in cases of accident and injury. They hope that after they enter Paradise, Allah will re-create them in such a fine form that it cannot be compared with their worldly bodies. This is their hoped-for reward for their steadfast patience when confronted with various difficulties. For this reason they do not forget that whatever they have suffered here will entitle them to a great recompense in the afterlife.

Those who are precluded from having faith, due to their attachment to the world, cannot show patience in the face of such events and so sink into great hopelessness and grief. For example, those with crippled limbs say that they would rather die than live with such a body; some even try to commit suicide. Believing that this life is the only one that they have, they think that living with certain defects and deficiencies makes life meaningless. Even if they do not try to commit suicide, they develop a very unpleasant personality and try to create problems for those around them. Whether they accept their situation or not, there is no way that they can avert such an event. If they put their trust in Allah, however, they may hope that He will allow them to be reborn in Paradise with a brand new body that is flawless, imperishable, and cannot be damaged. But if they do not trust in Allah, their present life and their future life in the Hereafter will be destroyed, for their ignorance will cause them to rebel against Allah and be "rewarded" with Hell.

The behavior of those who live the Qur'an's morality is completely different. When they are injured, lose an organ, or experience a similar disaster, their behavior does not change. Knowing that they are being tested and that the end result will be positive, they remain patient and do their best to earn Allah's approval. Even if they can no longer make any physical effort to realize this goal, they try to develop ideas that can benefit people and remind them of the Hereafter.

Those who turn away from Allah when they become ill or when they are injured are not aware of their great error, for only Allah can heal them or rescue them from their illness. Doctors, medicines, and treatments can be provided only with Allah's permission. Understanding this, the faithful face their illness with patience and patiently ask Him for a cure. They also make the best possible use of doctors, medicines, and treatments, and always remember that these will be of benefit only if Allah wills it.

The Qur'an gives the example of Prophet Ayyub (as), who always sought refuge in Allah when faced with illness. Allah praises his morality, as follows: **"We found him steadfast. What an excellent servant! He truly turned to his Lord"** (Surah Sad, 44). His patience and devotion to Allah are described, as follows:

And Ayyub, when he called out to his Lord, [said]: "Great harm has afflicted me, and You are the Most Merciful of the merciful." We responded to him and removed from him the harm that was afflicting him, restored his family to him and the same again with them, as a mercy direct from Us and a Reminder to all worshippers. (Surat al-Anbiya', 83-84)

The superior morality shown by Prophet Ayyub (as) when he was faced with this situation can be understood from his sincere prayer to Allah. When he was in trouble and sick, he turned to Allah with steadfastness and patience, knowing that only He can achieve anything and without forgetting that he is subject to Allah's mercy and compassion.

As we can see in these and all other cases, Allah helps those who are patient. One verse expresses this assistance, as follows:

And be steadfast. Allah is with the steadfast. (Surat al-Anfal, 46)

When facing injustice

Those who do not follow the Qur'an's morality cannot exercise true justice, because they do not consider that they will have to account for all of their actions in the afterlife, and so feel no need to be scrupulous in this matter. Since they follow their earthly desires rather than their consciences, they make impulsive, instead of rational, decisions. When they become angry, they immediately succumb to their anger and seek revenge. When a situation threatens their advantages, they do not hesitate to behave unjustly to protect their own interests. Such acts fill the newspapers and the television newscasts. Someone attacks his boss when he is fired, slanders somebody who has interfered with her business, spreads malicious gossip about his fiancée who broke up with him, or responds to a person who threatens her with even worse threats. We meet such people all the time. They respond to a bad act or an injustice in the same manner and violate the morality called for by the Qur'an. Indeed, sometimes people may even try to kill those who have interfered with their interests.

The faithful may be subjected to the unjust behavior of such people as part of their lifelong test. Unlike those given as examples above, they do not respond to injustice with injustice or to wrongdoing with more wrongdoing. But this does not mean that they stand by idly and do nothing to fight such injustice. However, rather than making rash decisions and jumping to conclusions, they act at all times in a well-balanced manner that comes from their trust in Allah.

Their patience and steadfastness in such cases springs from their awareness that Allah controls everything and possesses eternal justice. Allah tells us that on the Day of Judgment, everybody will have to account for what they did while in this world, and that no injustice will be done to them. Hence, those who committed injustice thoughtlessly or behaved in an unfair manner will receive their "reward" on that day. Allah's eternal justice is described, as follows:

We will set up the Just Balance on the Day of Rising, and no one will be wronged in any way. Even if it is no more than the weight of a grain of a mustard-seed, We will produce it. We are sufficient as a Reckoner. (Surat al-Anbiya', 47)

There are only grounds against those who wrong people and act as tyrants in the land without any right to do so. Such people will have a painful punishment. (Surat ash-Shura, 42)

Have fear of a Day when you will be returned to Allah. Then every self will be paid in full for what it earned. They will not be wronged. (Surat al-Baqara, 281)

Thus the faithful who know this law of Allah are patient in the face of injustice, thanks to the serenity that they have inside themselves. In the following verse, Allah promises that in exchange for this patience, He will bring help:

Allah will certainly help those who help Him—Allah is All-Strong, Almighty. (Surat al-Hajj, 40)

The Qur'an relates that Prophet Yusuf (as) faced many injustices throughout his life, but that because of his devotion and patience, Allah helped him and gave him strength. All that happened to him from his childhood onward was designed to test his patience and that of his father, Prophet Ya`qub (as). First, Prophet Yusuf (as) was thrown into a well by his jealous brothers. After this, a passing caravan found him and took him to Egypt, were he was sold as a slave. The Qur'an speaks of Prophet Ya`qub's (as) patience when confronted with this event, and of his request to Allah for help against this plot:

> They then produced his shirt with false blood on it. He [Ya`qub] said: "It is merely that your lower selves have suggested something to you which you did, but beauty lies in showing steadfastness. Allah alone is my Help in the face of the event you describe." (Surah Yusuf, 18)

In addition to this, Prophet Yusuf (as) was slandered by the wife of his master, the Egyptian vizier. Even though his innocence was perfectly clear, Prophet Yusuf (as) was thrown into prison, where he remained unjustly imprisoned for many years. However, he never forgot that Allah was testing him and so took refuge in Him, asked for His help, and exhibited outstanding patience. He did not forget that Allah will eventually confound the schemes of the unbelievers and that the faithful will be successful. In return for his steadfast devotion and patience, Allah gave him blessings that would please him both in this world and in the afterlife:

> The king said: "Bring him to me straight away, so that I may draw him very close to me." When he had spoken with him, he [the king] declared: "Today you are trusted, established in our sight." He [Yusuf] said: "Entrust the treasures of the land to me, for in truth I am a knowing guardian." Thus We established Yusuf in the land so that he could live in any place he pleased. We grant Our grace to anyone We will, and do not allow to go to waste the wage of any people who do good. But the wages of the

Hereafter are the best for people who believe and have done their duty. (Surah Yusuf, 54-57)

Years after these events, Allah brought Prophet Yusuf (as) face-to-face with his treacherous brothers. He stated his faith in Allah, despite the injustice that he had suffered, and the compassion that Allah showed him, as follows:

They asked: "Are you Yusuf?" He said: "I am indeed Yusuf, and this here is my brother. Allah has acted graciously to us. As for those who do their duty and are steadfast, Allah does not allow to go to waste the wage of any people who do good." (Surah Yusuf, 90)

All of this material related in the Qur'an about Prophet Yusuf (as) is an important example of the ultimate hidden causes that can be revealed by patience, because the help that Allah gave to him is equally available for those who are faithful. Allah thwarts the plots devised for the faithful and responds to the injustices committed against them.

Encountering slander and hurtful words

Allah says that among the tests believers may face are troubling statements made by the unbelievers, as follows:

You will hear many abusive words from those given the Book before you, and from those who are unbelievers. But if you are steadfast and guard against evil, that is the most resolute course to take. (Surah Al 'Imran, 186)

All Prophets throughout history have met with slander and accusations from the peoples to whom they were sent. In particular, the leaders of these people who deny faith take the lead in such behavior and try to incite the unbelievers against the believers. The

most important reason for this is that the true religion offers a moral code that may deprive them of some worldly advantages that they obtained by unjust means. Since they hold a superior position in their communities in terms of wealth, rank, and status, they can easily exploit their people and convince them that injustice and wrongdoing are reasonable.

The Qur'an's morality requires people to be honest, just, and helpful toward the poor. Thus, because these leaders regard this characteristic of the faith as a danger to their worldly interests, they attempt to blacken the reputation of the faithful who attempt to spread religious morality and thereby make them unsuccessful.

We can see one of the clearest examples of this in the behavior of Pharaoh, who enslaved and abused the children of Israel. Allah sent Prophet Musa (as) as a savior to these people, who were exploited and forced to work in very arduous conditions. Pharaoh, observing that the true religion instructed him to behave justly, mercifully, and with a good conscience toward the children of Israel, tried to discredit Prophet Musa (as) and his followers in the people's eyes. By doing this, he thought that nobody would respect the religion preached by Prophet Musa (as) and that a danger to his own interests would thereby be averted. He also hoped that such slander would destroy the believers' morale and that they might abandon their efforts to spread the faith. The Qur'an relates some of these slanders, as follows:

We sent Musa with Our Signs and clear authority to Pharaoh, Haman, and Qarun. But they said: "A lying magician." (Surat al-Mu'min, 23-24)

But he turned away with his forces, saying: "A magician or a madman!" (Surat adh-Dhariyat, 39)

What Pharaoh and his circle said to Prophet Musa (as) was not unique to them, for all Prophets and Messengers whom Allah sent to teach His religion face the same accusations of lying and sorcery, being madmen or poets, or seeking profit for themselves. The fact that the faithful always have the same insulting words thrown at them, regardless of time or place, is not coincidental. On the contrary, these are tests that Allah created to observe their patience and steadfastness.

The Qur'an tells us of such situations, as follows:

Equally, no Messenger came to those before them without their saying: "A magician or a madman!" (Surat adh-Dhariyat, 52)

Allah tells us that such insults were hurled at Prophet Muhammad (saas) and his Companions:

When they are told: "Believe in the way that the people believe," they exclaim: "What! Are we to believe in the way that fools believe?" No indeed! They are the fools, but they do not know it. (Surat al-Baqara, 13)

The ruling circle of those of his people who did not believe said: "We do not see you as anything but a human being like ourselves. We do not see anyone following you but the lowest of us, unthinkingly. We do not see you as superior to us. On the contrary, we consider you to be liars." (Surah Hud, 27)

They say: "You, to whom the Reminder [the Qur'an] has been sent down, are clearly mad." (Surat al-Hijr, 6)

They are surprised that a warner should come to them from among themselves. The unbelievers say: "This is a lying magician." (Surah Sad, 4)

When they were told, "There is no god but Allah," they were arrogant. They said, "Are we to forsake our gods for a mad poet?" (Surat as-Saffat, 35-36)

Faced with all of these slanders, Allah's Prophets and pious servants behaved with outstanding patience, took refuge in Him, and asked for His help. The Qur'an gives the following example of this:

Say: "Lord, judge with truth! Our Lord is the All-Merciful, the One Whose help is sought in the face of what you describe." (Surat al-Anbiya', 112)

In the Qur'an, Allah responds to the behavior of the unbelievers who seek to abuse the Prophets, as follows:

Remind them then! For, by the blessing of your Lord, you are neither a soothsayer nor a madman. (Surat at-Tur, 29)

Do not obey the unbelievers and hypocrites, and disregard their abuse of you. Put your trust in Allah. Allah suffices as a Protector. (Surat al-Ahzab, 48)

As stated above, Allah points out that He expects the faithful to live by the Qur'an's morality regardless of what difficulties they may encounter, and to keep advising and reminding people about the faith. Thus, the faithful ignore all such behavior and move forward with devotion, patience, and true knowledge. In fact, without knowing it, the unbelievers' behavior only strengthens the believers' faith and increases the joy and excitement they feel about their religion.

Proclaiming their religion

In the Qur'an, Allah informs us of the Prophets' life-long patience in order to show us how to live a life of superior morality. This is a great blessing for those who believe and seek the road to Him.

During their lives, the Prophets informed their household members and relatives, as well as the people at large, about Allah's religion. While inviting people to the true faith, every Prophet gained a number of enemies and suffered from their verbal and physical assaults. But such assaults could not weaken them; rather, they passed their whole lives showing patience and determination in preaching Allah's religion.

One of these Messengers was Prophet Ibrahim (as). Throughout his life, he was tested by various incidents that demanded patience. Despite all of the unfavorable incidents that Allah set before him, he always displayed devotion, submission, and great patience. For example, his people, who worshipped stone idols, tried to burn him alive for inviting them to the true faith and Allah, the One. The Qur'an recounts this test, as follows:

> They said: "We heard a young man mentioning them. They call him Ibrahim." They said: "Bring him before the people's eyes so they can be witnesses." (Surat al-Anbiya', 60-61)
> They said: "Build a pyre for him and fling him into the blaze!" They tried to outwit him, but We made them the lowest. He said: "I am going toward my Lord; He will be my guide." (Surat as-Saffat, 97-99)

As stated above, Prophet Ibrahim's (as) tribe wanted to cast him into the fire. However, in exchange for his display of patience and devotion, Allah protected him by ordering the fire to become "coolness and peace for him," as follows:

> We said: "Fire, be coolness and peace for Ibrahim!" They desired to trap him, but We made them the losers. (Surat al-Anbiya', 69-70)

This incident is a help to Allah's servants who are patient and steadfast for Him, and it is one of the finest examples of what great blessings our Lord can grant to Muslims in return for their patience.

Prophet Ibrahim's (as) life story contains many other examples of patience and devotion, for he continued to announce Allah's existence and invite people to embrace the true faith until the end of his life. Even though no member of his tribe responded to his call, Prophet Ibrahim (as) never abandoned his mission and thereby showed great patience. He obeyed Allah's instructions in this matter and, while showing great effort and determination, continued to summon people to the faith. We can see his sincerity in the following verse:

Remember when he said to his father: "Father, why do you worship that which can neither hear nor see and is of no use to you at all? Father, knowledge that never reached you has come to me, so follow me and I will guide you to the right path. Father, do not worship Satan. Satan was disobedient to the All-Merciful. Father, I am afraid that a punishment from the All-Merciful will afflict you, and turn you into a comrade of Satan." He said: "Do you forsake my gods, Ibrahim? If you do not stop, I will stone you. Keep away from me for a good long time." (Surah Maryam, 42-46)

Another Prophet who made a patient and determined effort to explain Allah's religion to his people was Prophet Nuh (as). He approached his people in many different ways, but could not make them believe. Even though his people rejected him and put a great deal of pressure on him to make him stop preaching Allah's religion, all of their efforts failed, for he remained patient and put all of his trust in Allah. The Qur'an proclaims his outstanding patience while communicating Allah's religion, as follows:

Before them, the people of Nuh denied the truth. They denied Our servant, saying: "He is madman," and he was driven away with jeers. (Surat al-Qamar, 9)

He said: "My Lord, I have called my people night and day, but

my calling has only made them more evasive. Indeed, every time I called them to Your forgiveness, they put their fingers in their ears, wrapped themselves up in their clothes, and were overweeningly arrogant. Then I called them openly. Then I addressed them publicly and privately." (Surah Nuh, 5-9)

Certainly these examples can teach a lesson to all Muslims today. By sending the Qur'an to inform us of these events, Allah instructs us never to abandon our patience and always to follow the Prophets' examples of patience.

So be steadfast as the Messengers, with firm resolve, were also steadfast. (Surat al-Ahqaf, 35)

Just as among the tribes of old, it is possible that now and in the future believers will encounter similar situations and people who know nothing of religion, deny the faith, and have only a limited ability to comprehend it. In every age there may be people who deny Allah's existence and the afterlife. Muslims are required to explain to all people His existence and the truth of creation without becoming tired of doing so. They may encounter people who say: "I'm an atheist and so reject Allah's existence," feigning ignorance of all of the truths or scientific proofs that have been explained to them. Or some people may be unable to save themselves from the negative effects of the surrounding ignorant society and thus find it hard to understand the truths that are explained to them. In such a situation, being steadfast in preaching religion by trying every method, like Prophet Nuh (as), and taking all kinds of risks, like Prophet Ibrahim (as), are very important forms of worship, because strong patience in explaining the faith may help some people see the light and be saved in the afterlife.

Believers undertake this important service with the sole intention of helping to improve the afterlife of those around them, and they carry it out with great patience and no expectation of reward in this world. Of course, Muslims will not go unrewarded for this sincere effort in this world or the next, which they undertake regardless of the real or potential obstacles. Even if their efforts do not cause one person to embrace the faith, Allah will give them beauty and serenity in this world and great rewards in the afterlife.

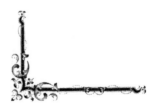

THE BENEFITS OF PATIENCE

Truly man is in loss—except for those who believe and do right actions and urge each other to the truth and steadfastness. (Surat al-'Asr, 2-3)

As Allah tells us in this verse, people who encourage one another to follow the truth and be steadfast receive various benefits. Patience develops people in many ways, such as allowing them to acquire superior morality, and offers them a beautiful and peaceful life that cannot be compared with the life of people who are far from the faith. In addition, believers have been promised greatly increased blessings in the afterlife in return for their patience. We list some of these fine and beautiful things, which are experienced in this world and the next, as follows:

Patience leads to intelligence

One of the major factors preventing people from acting intelligently is their impulsive thinking and behavior brought about by impatience. Sudden anger or desire shuts down the mind and pushes people to act without thinking. In the same way, such feelings as fear and irritation may prevent people from thinking logically and intelligently. People who do not live by the Qur'an's understanding of patience fall victim to such emotions for long periods of time and so become separated from intelligence.

However, the believers who always remain patient, as Allah counsels them, acquire great blessings, one of which is intelligence. As a result, they do not suffer from sudden fear, nervousness, or emotional excess. This enables them to evaluate all events in a calm and self-possessed manner and thereby arrive at the most intelligent conclusions and the most beneficial decisions.

Even more important, this patience allows the faithful to follow all of the Qur'an's teachings in the best possible way. Since believers always behave patiently, they have the opportunity to act only after evaluating events in light of the Qur'an's teaching. Those who follow the Qur'an are directed toward the true path of Allah and toward the finest behavior. For these reasons, following the Qur'an in the best possible way enables believers to gain the superior intelligence that derives from its wisdom.

Patience ensures subtle thought and the ability to see details

Another important characteristic of patience is that it enables the believers to see details that people cannot see right away, and thus helps them to use their intelligence. Impatient people want to solve everything right away and are not very interested in details. Consequently, they miss details that may be quite important and so make wrong decisions. In the same way, they cannot see the situation in which others around them find themselves, are incapable of noticing their needs, and so exhibit thoughtless behavior characterized by a lack of humaneness.

The faithful, always remaining patient, do not succumb to unnecessary haste while solving a problem. Understanding that haste is a primary factor of people's inability to use their intelligence and think correctly, they consider all details and make accurate decisions. Knowing how to act according to their intelligence without rushing, believers proceed intelligently, easily see those complexities that might be invisible to others, and thus adopt the most correct behavior.

Patience ensures the ability to do good

Patience enables people to overcome many of their bad characteristics and hence to discover good behavior. However, we must never forget that this is unique to believers. Those who do not fear Allah and forget that they will be recompensed in the afterlife for the morality they displayed in this world do not try to overcome their bad characteristics. As long as a worldly advantage is dangled in front of them, they can see no reason to alter their behavior. For example, if someone's elderly mother-in-law falls ill and that person has to move into her house to take care of her, he or she will need a great deal of patience. But those who cannot grasp the concept of Qur'anic patience can tolerate such a situation only for a short time. In a little while, that person begin to think ways of getting rid of this situation, and then says out loud: "Let's put her in a nursing home, because I can't look after her." Or an unbeliever's spouse has an accident, becomes bedridden, and requires intensive treatment and care. In such a situation, the other spouse will care for him or her for a while, perhaps to avoid the neighbors' criticism if they do not do so or for some other reason, but again only for a limited time. After this time, the spouse may abandon the other because he or she has no patience when it comes to self-sacrifice for others.

As for the faithful, they have an inner awe of Allah and know that they will find in the afterlife beauty and blessings commensurate to what they have done for Him. For this reason, they show determination and patience by always behaving well and making a serious effort. Thus they purge themselves of all bad characteristics and find the opportunity to turn these into good characteristics.

Patience ensures just behavior

By proclaiming that **"Allah commands you to return to their owners the things you hold on trust and, when you judge between people, to judge with justice. How excellent is what Allah exhorts you to do! Allah is All-Hearing, All-Seeing"** (Surat an-Nisa': 58), Allah states that He expects the faithful to behave justly. Aware of this command, the believers do not deviate from honesty and justice. In order for them to live this superior morality, their greatest aid is patience, a characteristic that they gain from adhering to the Qur'an's teachings.

Those who are expected to ensure justice must not give way to their emotions, succumb to anger, or act from such motives as hatred and revenge. When they encounter such a situation, they must display serious patience. Allah informs us of this, as follows:

O you who believe, show integrity for the sake of Allah, bearing witness with justice. Do not let hatred for a people incite you to injustice. Be just. That is closer to heedfulness. Heed Allah. Allah is aware of what you do. (Surat al-Ma'ida, 8)

Patience gives believers a trustworthy character

All Prophets have said these words to the peoples to whom they were sent:

Indeed, I am to you a trustworthy messenger. (Surat ash-Shu'ara', 143)

That they sought to define themselves in these terms as a priority arises from their awareness of just how important it is to be trustworthy in the people's eyes. This quality can be seen also in other believers, for adhering to the Qur'an's concept of superior morality and patience enables them to acquire all of the characteristics required for trustworthiness. In addition to patience, the believers also are intelligent, truthful, just, and moderate; free of hatred, anger, and untruthfulness; and balanced. Thus it is possible for people to know what the believers will do at any time and how they will react to events. While unbelievers exhibit an unbalanced character by reacting to events in unexpected, surprising, and disturbing ways, the faithful never behave in such a way. In fact, this is one of the reasons for their trustworthiness.

Most important, their continual patience at all times allows them to behave with determination in displaying this fine characteristic as long as they are alive. They make no concession to worldly profit in their behavior, a trait that pleases Allah. All of these elements together, along with living in a consistent manner, make the faithful the most trustworthy of all people.

Patience gives a person a cheerful and peaceful character

For people who have no faith in Allah, being sad, bored, or upset is a quite normal condition, for they ignore the facts that Allah controls everyone and everything, creates all events for a reason, can answer our prayers to Him whenever He wills to do so, and keeps everything in His power. Unaware of these truths, such people react to an apparently unfavorable development by immediately giving way to hopelessness and sorrow. The Qur'an mentions this characteristic of the unbelievers, as follows:

When We give people a taste of mercy, they rejoice in it. But when something bad happens to them because of what they themselves have done, they immediately lose all hope. (Surat ar-Rum, 36)

The faithful, on the other hand, never lose their hope in Allah, for He has infinite power and keeps everything in the universe under His control. He is the Friend, Guardian, and Helper of the faithful. He protects, guards, and gives ease to those who take refuge in Him.

The believers who can appreciate Allah's greatness and boundless mercy take refuge in Him with patience and trust, regardless of the difficulties, problems, or events that they may be experiencing. As a result, they never lose any of their cheerfulness and tranquility, even when experiencing their most difficult moments, for they know that Allah will give them a fine recompense in Paradise for the patience they displayed in this world. Therefore, they live their lives in great joy and enthusiasm.

Those who cannot show patience when confronted with adversities are condemned to spend their worldly lives in unhappiness. Allah points out that they will be unhappy in the afterlife as well. The Qur'an describes the rewards that those who are patient (the believers) and those who are impatient and therefore rebellious toward Allah (the unbelievers) will receive in the afterlife, as follows:

On the Day it comes, no one will speak except with His permission. Some of them will be wretched and others will be glad. As for those who are wretched, they will be in the Fire,

where they will sigh and gasp, remaining in it timelessly, forever, as long as the heavens and Earth endure, except as your Lord wills. Your Lord is the Doer of what He wills. As for those who are glad, they will be in Paradise, remaining in it timelessly, forever, as long as the heavens and Earth endure, except as your Lord wills. An uninterrupted gift. (Surah Hud, 105-108)

The wonderful life Allah promises to the faithful

Throughout this book, we have stated that Allah tests the faithful in various ways. However, this should not be taken to mean that they live difficult or troubled lives. On the contrary, the faithful live the best lives in this world because Allah places serenity and peace in their hearts on account of their continuous patience and devotion. This blessing is exclusive to the faithful, for it cannot be obtained with money or status, or by means of any of the other opportunities that the world has to offer. So many people who appear to be living in comfort feel none of the serenity and peace that Allah grants to the patient. They could not feel such feelings even if they somehow managed to offer all of the wealth in the world or mobilize all of its resources, because Allah places these feelings only in the hearts of the faithful:

He sent down serenity into the hearts of the believers, thereby increasing their faith with more faith—the legions of the heavens and Earth belong to Allah. Allah is All-Knowing, All-Wise. (Surat al-Fath, 4)

As a result, the believers never succumb to worry, concern, or unhappiness when they encounter difficulty and hardship.

In return for their unconditional submission, patience, and pleasant acceptance of everything that our Lord sends to them, Allah tells them that He will give them a beautiful life in the world:

Anyone who acts rightly, male or female, being a believer, We will give them a good life and recompense them according to the best of what they did. (Surat an-Nahl, 97)

As for those who do their duty and are steadfast, Allah does not allow to go to waste the wage of any people who do good. (Surah Yusuf, 90)

When those who have done their duty are asked: "What has your Lord sent down?" their reply is: "Good!" There is good in this world for those who do good, and the abode of the Hereafter is even better. How wonderful is the abode of those who guard against evil. (Surat an-Nahl, 30)

Say: "Servants of Mine who believe, heed your Lord. For those who do good in this world there is good, and Allah's Earth is spacious. The steadfast will be paid their wages in full without any reckoning." (Surat az-Zumar, 10)

The believers' reward for being patient is Paradise

People who are bound to Allah in their hearts dedicate their goods and lives, in short everything they own, to our Lord and are patient in order to earn His approval in both good and bad times. None of the troubles, pressures, and difficulties they experience in this world can prevent them from living according to Allah's religion, because they are devoted firmly and only to Him and show patience and determination for as long as they live.

The finest reward that the faithful can obtain in the afterlife for this outstanding patience is Allah's love, generosity, and approval:

Allah has promised the male and female believers Gardens with rivers flowing under them, remaining in them timelessly, forever, and fine dwellings in the Gardens of Eden. And Allah's good pleasure is even greater. That is the great victory. (Surat at-Tawba, 72)

Their Lord gives them the good news of His mercy, good pleasure, and Gardens in which they will enjoy everlasting delight. (Surat at-Tawba, 21)

Their reward is with their Lord: Gardens of Eden with rivers flowing under them, remaining in them timelessly, forever and ever. Allah is pleased with them, and they are pleased with Him. That is for those who fear their Lord. (Surat al-Bayyina, 8)

Allah's patient servants will be met in a Paradise of boundless beauty due to the angels' greetings of peace and good wishes, and through all eternity they will never leave it. Angels announce that these eternal blessings are the reward for their patience, as follows:

Gardens of Eden that they will enter, and all of their parents, wives, and children who were righteous. Angels will enter in to welcome them from every gate: "Peace be upon you because of your steadfastness! How wonderful is the Ultimate Abode!" (Surat ar-Ra'd, 23-24)

To those people who display a great determination to exhibit a fine morality throughout their lives, remaining steadfast in times of difficulty, and exhibiting behavior pleasing to Him, Allah multiplies their rewards many times over:

They will be given their reward twice over, because they have been steadfast... (Surat al-Qasas, 54)

Those believers regarded as worthy of Paradise will find there everything that their hearts desire. They will live in eye-catching mansions, sitting on couches of striking beauty and exquisite quilts and rugs, and will be together forever with the Prophets and the righteous believers. This is a definite reality that Allah has promised to believers in return for their patience. For these reasons, He calls upon them to compete for His approval and for Paradise while living in this world: **"Race each other to forgiveness from your Lord and a Garden [i.e., Paradise] as wide as the heavens and Earth, prepared for the people who guard against evil"** (Surah Al 'Imran, 133). In other verses, He brings the good news to the faithful, as follows:

> **Such people will be repaid for their steadfastness with the Highest Paradise, where they will meet with welcome and with "Peace." (Surat al-Furqan, 75)**
>
> **Today I have rewarded them for being steadfast. They are the ones who are victorious. (Surat al-Mu'minun, 111)**

THE SECRETS OF PATIENCE

> *... And be steadfast. Allah is with the steadfast. (Surat al-Anfal, 46)*

The Qur'an guides people to the ways of peace and teaches them what they previously did not know. It informs them of all the secrets of worldly life and the afterlife. One of the secrets that people can learn only from it is patience. Patience is not just one part of upstanding morality; rather, it is an important path by which the faithful are guided to Allah's mercy.

Allah grants unexpected blessings to His faithful servants who show patience while dealing with the troubles that befall them and who live in full the Qur'an's morality and carry out His commands.

The Qur'an informs us of Allah's promised blessings to Muslims who show patience, as follows:

In showing patience, small communities may, with Allah's permission, defeat large communities

When Talut marched out with the army, he said: "Allah will test you with a river. Anyone who drinks from it is not with me. But anyone who does not taste it is with me—except for him who merely scoops up a little in his hand." But they drank from it—except for a few of them. Then when he and those who believed with him had crossed it, they said: "We do not have the strength to face Goliath and his troops today." But those who were sure that they were going to meet Allah said: "How many a small force has triumphed over a much greater one by Allah's permission! Allah is with the steadfast." (Surat al-Baqara, 249)

Traps cannot harm those who remain steadfast and guard against evil

If something good happens to you, it galls them. If something bad strikes you, they rejoice at it. But if you are steadfast and guard against evil, their scheming will not harm you in any way. Allah encompasses what they do. (Surah Al 'Imran, 120)

Allah promises to aid His servants, who are steadfast and guard against evil, with His angels

Yes indeed! But if you are steadfast and guard against evil, and they come upon you suddenly, your Lord will reinforce you with five thousand angels, clearly identified. (Surah Al 'Imran, 125)

Allah multiplies the strength of the faithful

O Prophet! Spur on the believers to fight. If twenty of you are steadfast, they will overcome two hundred; and if there are a hundred of you, they will overcome a thousand of those who do not believe, because they are people who do not understand. Now Allah has made it lighter on you, knowing that there is weakness in you. If a hundred of you are steadfast, they will overcome two hundred; and if there are a thousand of you, they will overcome two thousand with Allah's permission. Allah is with the steadfast. (Surat al-Anfal, 65-66)

Allah keeps His promises to the patient

And We bequeathed to the people who had been oppressed the easternmost part of the land We had blessed, and its westernmost part as well. The most excellent Word of your Lord was fulfilled for the tribe of Israel on account of their steadfastness. And We utterly destroyed what Pharaoh and his people made and the buildings they constructed. (Surat al-A'raf, 137)

THE PRAYERS OF THE FAITHFUL FOR PATIENCE

Musa said to his people: "Seek help in Allah and be steadfast. Earth belongs to Allah. He bequeaths it to any of His servants He wills. The successful outcome is for those who guard against evil." (Surat al-A'raf, 128)

In one verse, **"If My servants ask you about Me, I am near. I answer the call of the caller when he calls on Me. They should therefore respond to Me and believe in Me so that hopefully they will be rightly guided"** (Surat al-Baqara, 186), Allah calls upon the faithful to pray to Him about anything because He loves His servants and has mercy on them. When His servants fall into trouble, Allah eases their lot and brings them peace. The Qur'an speaks of Allah's help to the faithful, as follows:

He calls down blessing on you, as do His angels, to bring you out of the darkness into the light. He is Most Merciful to believers. (Surat al-Ahzab, 43)

The faithful, who realize what an important place patience has in living a moral life and carrying out Allah's instructions, pray to Him about everything, including patience. They know that patience is a blessing that can solve all kinds of problems, directs them toward the true path, and, most importantly, earns them Allah's love and Paradise.

The Prayers Of The Faithful For Patience

The Qur'an contains prayers of the faithful informing Allah that they desire patience. By asking Him to "pour down steadfastness upon us," they draw attention to the greatness of people's need for patience:

You are only avenging yourself on us because we believed in our Lord's Signs when they came to us. Our Lord, pour down steadfastness upon us and take us back to You as Muslims. (Surat al-A'raf, 126)

When they came out against Talut and his troops, they said: "Our Lord, pour down steadfastness upon us, make our feet firm, and help us against this unbelieving people." (Surat al-Baqara, 250)

The believers' prayers for patience, as recorded in the Qur'an, also remind us of how necessary it is to ask for Allah's help in this matter. Right from the beginning of this book, we have stressed that Allah helps those who are patient and who patiently ask for His help, and that He has promised to multiply their blessings. One of the most important characteristics that a person needs is patience, so that he or she can confront all of this life's difficulties, problems, and troubles with the joy of faith and the excitement of earning Allah's approval. These inner characteristics help the believer to have the upper hand, with Allah's permission, and ensure their success. Allah has given this secret of patience to the faithful and told them to be patient, pray for patience, and display patience.

CONCLUSION

In one verse, Allah describes the believers with these words: **"Those who listen well to what is said and follow the best of it, they are the ones whom Allah has guided, they are the people of intelligence"** (Surat az-Zumar, 18). Truly the faithful have intelligence and, consequently, heed His words and do their best.

In addition, we have used various examples from the Qur'an to point out that patience is one of the most important elements forming the foundation of superior morality and opening the door to countless blessings in this world and the next. We have invited all people of intelligence to be patient, in the full Qur'anic meaning of the word, and have brought the good news that people who adhere to morality and who always display a strong patience in order to earn Allah's approval will be rewarded in this world and in the afterlife.

Now, after all of these explanations, we conclude by reminding the readers that the finest reward a person can obtain in this world and the next is Allah's approval and mercy, and His Paradise. Such wonders cannot be compared with any of this world's pleasures and blessings. One way of gaining His love is to be aware of Allah's wisdom and bounty in every event, word, and act, and to trust in Allah, for the Qur'an tells us that He loves those who trust Him and show patience in all circumstances:

How many of the Prophets fought [in Allah's way], and with them [fought] large bands of godly men? But they never lost heart if they met with disaster in Allah's way, nor did they weaken (in will) or give in. And Allah loves those who are firm

and steadfast. (Surah Al 'Imran, 146)

For these reasons, Allah declares that the faithful should race each other to acquire this morality: **"O you who believe, persevere in patience and constancy, vie in such perseverance; strengthen each other, and heed Allah, so that hopefully you will be successful"** (Surah Al 'Imran, 200).

In addition, remember that life comes and goes just as quickly for those who live morally as for those who do not. Those who exhibit impatience when facing the tests that Allah creates while they are in this world, who revolt against them by becoming impatient, and who are not constant in their morality and worship one day will die and find themselves between Heaven and Hell. Those who choose patience and surrender to Destiny spend their temporary life here in the finest possible way and will enter Paradise due to their trust in Allah. Those who spend their life being impatient, and complaining about their difficulties and troubles will find themselves in the darkness of Hell, just as they lived here in the darkness of irreligion, and will realize that they have sacrificed eternal life for a short temporary life on Earth.

This book seeks to warn such people before that day comes and before they say with great regret: **"If only we had really listened and used our intellect, we would not have been Companions of the Blaze"** (Surat al-Mulk, 10). It also invites everybody to live in the patience, which opens the way to all good things, and to vie with others in living this morality.

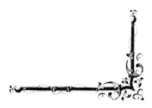

THE DECEPTION OF EVOLUTION

Darwinism, in other words the theory of evolution, was put forward with the aim of denying the fact of creation, but is in truth nothing but failed, unscientific nonsense. This theory, which claims that life emerged by chance from inanimate matter, was invalidated by the scientific evidence of clear "design" in the universe and in living things. In this way, science confirmed the fact that Allah created the universe and the living things in it. The propaganda carried out today in order to keep the theory of evolution alive is based solely on the distortion of the scientific facts, biased interpretation, and lies and falsehoods disguised as science.

Yet this propaganda cannot conceal the truth. The fact that the theory of evolution is the greatest deception in the history of science has been expressed more and more in the scientific world over the last 20-30 years. Research carried out after the 1980s in particular has revealed that the claims of Darwinism are totally unfounded, something that has been stated by a large number of scientists. In the United States in particular, many scientists from such different fields as biology, biochemistry and paleontology recognize the invalidity of Darwinism and employ the concept of intelligent design to account for the origin of life. This "intelligent design" is a scientific expression of the fact that Allah created all living things.

We have examined the collapse of the theory of evolution and the proofs of creation in great scientific detail in many of our works, and are still continuing to do so. Given the enormous importance of this subject, it will be of great benefit to summarize it here.

The Scientific Collapse of Darwinism

Although this doctrine goes back as far as ancient Greece, the theory of evolution was advanced extensively in the nineteenth century. The most important development that made it the top topic of the world of science was Charles Darwin's **The Origin of Species**, published in 1859. In this book, he denied that Allah created different living species on Earth separately, for he claimed that all living beings had a common ancestor and had diversified over time through small changes. Darwin's theory was not based on any concrete scientific finding; as he also accepted, it was just an "assumption." Moreover, as Darwin confessed in the long chapter of his book titled "Difficulties of the Theory," the theory failed in the face of many critical questions.

Darwin invested all of his hopes in new scientific discoveries, which he expected to solve these difficulties. However, contrary to his expectations, scientific findings expanded the dimensions of these difficulties. The defeat of Darwinism in the face of science can be reviewed under three basic topics:

1) The theory cannot explain how life originated on Earth.

2) No scientific finding shows that the "evolutionary mechanisms" proposed by the theory have any evolutionary power at all.

3) The fossil record proves the exact opposite of what the theory suggests

In this section, we will examine these three basic points in general outlines:

The First Insurmountable Step: The Origin of Life

The theory of evolution posits that all living species evolved from a single living cell that emerged on the primitive Earth 3.8 billion years ago. How a single cell could generate millions of complex living species and, if such an evolution really occurred, why traces of it cannot be observed in the fossil record are some of the questions that the theory cannot answer. However, first and foremost, we need to ask: How did this "first cell" originate?

Since the theory of evolution denies creation and any kind of supernatural intervention, it maintains that the "first cell" originated coincidentally within the laws of nature, without any design, plan or arrangement. According to the theory, inanimate matter must have produced a living cell as a result of coincidences. Such a claim, however, is inconsistent with the most unassailable rules of biology.

"Life Comes from Life"

In his book, Darwin never referred to the origin of life. The primitive understanding of science in his time rested on the assumption that living beings had a very simple structure. Since medieval times, spontaneous generation, which asserts that non-living materials came together to form living organisms, had been widely accepted. It was commonly believed that insects came into being from food leftovers, and mice from wheat. Interesting experiments were conducted to prove this theory. Some wheat was placed on a dirty piece of cloth, and it was believed that mice would originate from it after a while.

Similarly, maggots developing in rotting meat was assumed to be evidence of spontaneous generation. However, it was later understood that worms did not appear on meat spontaneously, but were carried there by flies in the form of larvae, invisible to the naked eye.

Even when Darwin wrote *The Origin of Species*, the belief that bacteria could come into existence from non-living matter was widely accepted in the world of science.

However, five years after the publication of Darwin's book, Louis Pasteur announced his results after long studies and experiments, that disproved spontaneous generation, a cornerstone of Darwin's theory. In his triumphal lecture at the Sorbonne in 1864, Pasteur said: "Never will the doctrine of spontaneous generation recover from the mortal blow struck by this simple experiment."[1]

For a long time, advocates of the theory of evolution resisted these findings. However, as the development of science unraveled the complex structure of the cell of a living being, the idea that life could come into being coincidentally faced an even greater impasse.

Inconclusive Efforts in the Twentieth Century

The first evolutionist who took up the subject of the origin of life in the twentieth century was the renowned Russian biologist Alexander Oparin. With various theses he advanced in the 1930s, he tried to prove that a living cell could originate by coincidence. These studies, however, were doomed to failure, and Oparin had to make the following confession:

Unfortunately, however, the problem of the origin of the cell is perhaps the most obscure point in the whole study of the evolution of organisms.[2]

Evolutionist followers of Oparin tried to carry out experiments to solve this problem. The best known experiment was carried out by the American chemist Stanley Miller in 1953. Combining the gases he alleged to have existed in the primordial Earth's atmosphere in an experiment set-up, and adding energy to the mixture, Miller synthesized several organic molecules (amino acids) present in the structure of proteins.

76 THE IMPORTANCE OF PATIENCE IN THE QUR'AN

Barely a few years had passed before it was revealed that this experiment, which was then presented as an important step in the name of evolution, was invalid, for the atmosphere used in the experiment was very different from the real Earth conditions.[3]

After a long silence, Miller confessed that the atmosphere medium he used was unrealistic.[4]

All the evolutionists' efforts throughout the twentieth century to explain the origin of life ended in failure. The geochemist Jeffrey Bada, from the San Diego Scripps Institute accepts this fact in an article published in *Earth* magazine in 1998:

> *Today as we leave the twentieth century, we still face the biggest unsolved problem that we had when we entered the twentieth century: How did life originate on Earth?*[5]

The Complex Structure of Life

The primary reason why the theory of evolution ended up in such a great impasse regarding the origin of life is that even those living organisms deemed to be the simplest have incredibly complex structures. The cell of a living thing is more complex than all of our man-made technological products. Today, even in the most developed laboratories of the world, a living cell cannot be produced by bringing organic chemicals together.

The conditions required for the formation of a cell are too great in quantity to be explained away by coincidences. The probability of proteins, the building blocks of a cell, being synthesized coincidentally, is 1 in 10950 for an average protein made up of 500 amino acids. In mathematics, a probability smaller than 1 over 1050 is considered to be impossible in practical terms.

The DNA molecule, which is located in the nucleus of a cell and which stores genetic information, is an incredible databank. If the information coded in DNA were written down, it would make a giant library consisting of an estimated 900 volumes of encyclopedias consisting of 500 pages each.

A very interesting dilemma emerges at this point: DNA can replicate itself only with the help of some specialized proteins (enzymes). However, the synthesis of these enzymes can be realized only by the information coded in DNA. As they both depend on each other, they have to exist at the same time for replication. This brings the scenario that life originated by itself to a deadlock. Prof. Leslie Orgel, an evolutionist of repute from the University of San Diego, California, confesses this fact in the September 1994 issue of the *Scientific American* magazine:

> *It is extremely improbable that proteins and nucleic acids, both of which are structurally complex, arose spontaneously in the same place at the same time. Yet it also seems impossible to have one without the other. And so, at first glance, one might have to conclude that life could never, in fact, have originated by chemical means.*[6]

No doubt, if it is impossible for life to have originated from natural causes, then it has to be accepted that life was "created" in a supernatural way. This fact explicitly invalidates the theory of evolution, whose main purpose is to deny creation.

Imaginary Mechanisms of Evolution

The second important point that negates Darwin's theory is that both concepts put forward by the theory as "evolutionary mechanisms" were understood to have, in reality, no evolutionary power.

Darwin based his evolution allegation entirely on the mechanism of "natural selection." The importance he placed on this mechanism was evident in the name of his book: *The Origin of Species, By Means of Natural Selection...*

Natural selection holds that those living things that are stronger and more suited to the natural conditions of their habitats will survive in the struggle for life. For example, in a deer herd under the threat of attack by wild animals, those that can run faster will survive. Therefore, the deer herd will be comprised of faster and stronger individuals. However, unquestionably, this mechanism will not cause deer to evolve and transform themselves into another living species, for instance, horses.

Therefore, the mechanism of natural selection has no evolutionary power. Darwin was also aware of this fact and had to state this in his book *The Origin of Species:*

> *Natural selection can do nothing until favourable individual differences or variations occur.*[7]

Lamarck's Impact

So, how could these "favorable variations" occur? Darwin tried to answer this question from the standpoint of the primitive understanding of science at that time. According to the French biologist Chevalier de Lamarck (1744-1829), who lived before Darwin, living creatures passed on the traits they acquired during their lifetime to the next generation. He asserted that these traits, which accumulated from one generation to another, caused new species to be formed. For instance, he claimed that giraffes evolved from antelopes; as they struggled to eat the leaves of high trees, their necks were extended from generation to generation.

Darwin also gave similar examples. In his book *The Origin of Species*, for instance, he said that some bears going into water to find food transformed themselves into whales over time.[8]

However, the laws of inheritance discovered by Gregor Mendel (1822-84) and verified by the science of genetics, which flourished in the twentieth century, utterly demolished the legend that acquired traits were passed on to subsequent generations. Thus, natural selection fell out of favor as an evolutionary mechanism.

Neo-Darwinism and Mutations

In order to find a solution, Darwinists advanced the "Modern Synthetic Theory," or as it is more commonly known, Neo-Darwinism, at the end of the 1930's. Neo-Darwinism added mutations, which are distortions formed in the genes of living beings due to such external factors as radiation or replication errors, as the "cause of favorable variations" in addition to natural mutation.

Today, the model that stands for evolution in the world is Neo-Darwinism. The theory maintains that millions of living beings formed as a result of a process whereby numerous complex organs of these organisms (e.g., ears, eyes, lungs, and wings) underwent "mutations," that is, genetic disorders. Yet, there is an outright scientific fact that totally undermines this theory: Mutations do not cause living beings to develop; on the contrary, they are always harmful.

The reason for this is very simple: DNA has a very complex structure, and random effects can only harm it. The American geneticist B.G. Ranganathan explains this as follows:

First, genuine mutations are very rare in nature. Secondly, most mutations are harmful since they are random, rather than orderly changes in the structure of genes; any random change in a highly ordered system will be for the worse, not for the better. For example, if an earthquake were to shake a highly ordered structure such as a building, there would be a random change in the framework of the building which, in all probability, would not be an improvement.[9]

Not surprisingly, no mutation example, which is useful, that is, which is observed to develop the genetic code, has been observed so far. All mutations have proved to be harmful. It was understood that mutation, which is presented as an "evolutionary mechanism," is actually a genetic occurrence that harms living things, and leaves them disabled. (The most common effect of mutation on human beings is cancer.) Of course, a destructive mechanism cannot be an "evolutionary mechanism." Natural selection, on the other hand, "can do nothing by itself," as Darwin also accepted. This fact shows us that there is no "evolutionary mechanism" in nature. Since no evolutionary mechanism exists, no such any imaginary process called "evolution" could have taken place.

The Fossil Record: No Sign of Intermediate Forms

The clearest evidence that the scenario suggested by the theory of evolution did not take place is the fossil record.

According to this theory, every living species has sprung from a predecessor. A previously existing species turned into something else over time and all species have come into being in this way. In other words, this transformation proceeds gradually over millions of years.

Had this been the case, numerous intermediary species should have existed and lived within this long transformation period.

For instance, some half-fish/half-reptiles should have lived in

The Deception Of Evolution   *81*

the past which had acquired some reptilian traits in addition to the fish traits they already had. Or there should have existed some reptile-birds, which acquired some bird traits in addition to the reptilian traits they already had. Since these would be in a transitional phase, they should be disabled, defective, crippled living beings. Evolutionists refer to these imaginary creatures, which they believe to have lived in the past, as "transitional forms."

If such animals ever really existed, there should be millions and even billions of them in number and variety. More importantly, the remains of these strange creatures should be present in the fossil record. In *The Origin of Species*, Darwin explained:

> *If my theory be true, numberless intermediate varieties, linking most closely all of the species of the same group together must assuredly have existed.... Consequently, evidence of their former existence could be found only amongst fossil remains.*[10]

Darwin's Hopes Shattered

However, although evolutionists have been making strenuous efforts to find fossils since the middle of the nineteenth century all over the world, no transitional forms have yet been uncovered. All of the fossils, contrary to the evolutionists' expectations, show that life appeared on Earth all of a sudden and fully-formed.

One famous British paleontologist, Derek V. Ager, admits this fact, even though he is an evolutionist:

> *The point emerges that if we examine the fossil record in detail, whether at the level of orders or of species, we find—over and over again—not gradual evolution, but the sudden explosion of one group*

at the expense of another.[11]

This means that in the fossil record, all living species suddenly emerge as fully formed, without any intermediate forms in between. This is just the opposite of Darwin's assumptions. Also, this is very strong evidence that all living things are created. The only explanation of a living species emerging suddenly and complete in every detail without any evolutionary ancestor is that it was created. This fact is admitted also by the widely known evolutionist biologist Douglas Futuyma:

> *Creation and evolution, between them, exhaust the possible explanations for the origin of living things. Organisms either appeared on the earth fully developed or they did not. If they did not, they must have developed from pre-existing species by some process of modification. If they did appear in a fully developed state, they must indeed have been created by some omnipotent intelligence.*[12]

Fossils show that living beings emerged fully developed and in a perfect state on the Earth. That means that "the origin of species," contrary to Darwin's supposition, is not evolution, but creation.

The Tale of Human Evolution

The subject most often brought up by advocates of the theory of evolution is the subject of the origin of man. The Darwinist claim holds that modern man evolved from ape-like creatures. During this alleged evolutionary process, which is supposed to have started 4-5 million years ago, some "transitional forms" between modern man and his ancestors are supposed to have existed. According to this completely imaginary scenario, four basic "categories" are listed:

1. *Australopithecus*
2. *Homo habilis*
3. *Homo erectus*
4. *Homo sapiens*

Evolutionists call man's so-called first ape-like ancestors *Australopithecus*, which means "South African ape." These living beings are actually nothing but an old ape species that has become extinct. Extensive research done on various *Australopithecus* specimens by two world famous anatomists from England and the USA, namely, Lord Solly Zuckerman and Prof. Charles Oxnard, shows that these apes belonged to an ordinary ape species that became extinct and bore no resemblance to humans.[13]

Evolutionists classify the next stage of human evolution as "*homo*," that is "man." According to their claim, the living beings in the *Homo* series are more developed than *Australopithecus*. Evolutionists devise a fanciful evolution scheme by arranging different fossils of these creatures in a particular order. This scheme is imaginary because it has never been proved that there is an evolutionary relation between these different classes. Ernst Mayr, one of the twentieth century's most important evolutionists, contends in his book *One Long Argument* that "particularly historical [puzzles] such as the origin of life or of *Homo sapiens*, are extremely difficult and may even resist a final, satisfying explanation."[14]

By outlining the link chain as *Australopithecus* > *Homo habilis* > *Homo erectus* > *Homo sapiens*, evolutionists imply that each of these species is one another's ancestor. However, recent findings of paleoanthropologists have revealed that *Australopithecus, Homo habilis,* and *Homo erectus* lived at different parts of the world at the same time.[15]

Moreover, a certain segment of humans classified as *Homo erectus* have lived up until very modern times. *Homo sapiens neandarthalensis* and *Homo sapiens sapiens* (modern man) co-existed in the same region.[16]

This situation apparently indicates the invalidity of the claim that they are ancestors of one another. A paleontologist from Harvard University, Stephen Jay Gould, explains this deadlock of the theory of evolution, although he is an evolutionist himself:

> *What has become of our ladder if there are three coexisting lineages of hominids (A. africanus, the robust australopithecines, and H. habilis), none clearly derived from another? Moreover, none of the three display any evolutionary trends during their tenure on earth.*[17]

Put briefly, the scenario of human evolution, which is "upheld" with the help of various drawings of some "half ape, half human" creatures appearing in the media and course books, that is, frankly, by means of propaganda, is nothing but a tale with no scientific foundation.

Lord Solly Zuckerman, one of the most famous and respected scientists in the U.K., who carried out research on this subject for years and studied *Australopithecus* fossils for 15 years, finally concluded, despite being an evolutionist himself, that there is, in fact, no such family tree branching out from ape-like creatures to man.

Zuckerman also made an interesting "spectrum of science" ranging from those he considered scientific to those he considered unscientific. According to Zuckerman's spectrum, the most "scientific"—that is, depending on concrete data—fields of science are chemistry and physics. After them come the biological sciences and then the social sciences. At the far end of the spectrum, which is the part considered to be most "unscientific," are "extra-sensory perception"—concepts such as telepathy and sixth sense—and finally "human evolution." Zuckerman explains his reasoning:

> We then move right off the register of objective truth into those fields of presumed biological science, like extrasensory perception or the interpretation of man's fossil history, where to the faithful [evolutionist] anything is possible—and where the ardent believer [in evolution] is sometimes able to believe several contradictory things at the same time.[18]

The tale of human evolution boils down to nothing but the prejudiced interpretations of some fossils unearthed by certain people, who blindly adhere to their theory.

Technology in the Eye and the Ear

Another subject that remains unanswered by evolutionary theory is the excellent quality of perception in the eye and the ear.

Before passing on to the subject of the eye, let us briefly answer the question of how we see. Light rays coming from an object fall oppositely on the eye's retina. Here, these light rays are transmitted into electric signals by cells and reach a tiny spot at the back of the brain, the "center of vision." These electric signals are perceived in this center as an image after a series of processes. With this technical background, let us do some thinking.

The brain is insulated from light. That means that its inside is completely dark, and that no light reaches the place where it is located. Thus, the "center of vision" is never touched by light and may even be the darkest place you have ever known. However, you observe a luminous, bright world in this pitch darkness.

The image formed in the eye is so sharp and distinct that even the technology of the twentieth century has not been able to attain it. For instance, look at the book you are reading, your hands with which you are holding it, and then lift your head and look around you. Have you ever seen such a sharp and distinct image as this one at any other place? Even the most developed television screen produced by the greatest television producer in the world cannot provide such a sharp image for you. This is a three-dimensional, colored, and extremely sharp image. For more than 100 years, thousands of engineers have been trying to achieve this sharpness. Factories, huge premises were established, much research has been done, plans and designs have been made for this purpose. Again, look at a TV screen and the book you hold in your hands. You will see that there is a big difference in sharpness and distinction. Moreover, the TV screen shows you a two-dimensional image, whereas with your eyes, you watch a three-dimensional perspective with depth.

For many years, tens of thousands of engineers have tried to make a three-dimensional TV and achieve the vision quality of the eye. Yes, they have made a three-dimensional television system, but it is not possible to watch it without putting on special 3-D glasses; moreover, it is only an artificial three-dimension. The background is more blurred, the foreground appears like a paper setting. Never has it been possible to produce a sharp and distinct vision like that of the eye. In both the camera and the television, there is a loss of image quality.

Evolutionists claim that the mechanism producing this sharp and distinct image has been formed by chance. Now, if somebody told you that the television in your room was formed as a result of chance, that all of its atoms just happened to come together and make up this device that produces an image, what would you think? How can atoms do what thousands of people cannot?

If a device producing a more primitive image than the eye could not have been formed by chance, then it is very evident that the eye and the image seen by the eye could not have been formed by chance. The same situation applies to the ear. The outer ear picks up the available sounds by the auricle and directs them to the middle ear, the middle ear transmits the sound vibrations by intensifying them, and the inner ear sends these vibrations to the brain by translating them into electric signals. Just as with the eye, the act of hearing finalizes in the center of hearing in the brain.

The situation in the eye is also true for the ear. That is, the brain is insulated from sound just as it is from light. It does not let any sound in. Therefore, no matter how noisy is the outside, the inside of the brain is completely silent. Nevertheless, the sharpest sounds are perceived in the brain. In your completely silent brain, you listen to symphonies, and hear all of the noises in a crowded place. However, were the sound level in your brain was measured by a precise device at that moment, complete silence would be found to be prevailing there.

As is the case with imagery, decades of effort have been spent in trying to generate and reproduce sound that is faithful to the original. The results of these efforts are sound recorders, high-fidelity systems, and systems for sensing sound. Despite all of this technology and the thousands of engineers and experts who have been working on this endeavor, no sound has yet been obtained that has the same sharpness and clarity as the sound perceived by the ear. Think of the highest-quality hi-fi systems produced by the largest company in the music industry. Even in these devices, when sound is recorded some of it is lost; or when you turn on a hi-fi you always hear a hissing sound before the music starts. However, the sounds that are the products of the human body's technology are extremely sharp and clear. A human ear never perceives a sound accompanied by a hissing sound or with atmospherics as does a hi-fi; rather, it perceives sound exactly as it is, sharp and clear. This is the way it has been since the creation of man.

So far, no man-made visual or recording apparatus has been as sensitive and successful in perceiving sensory data as are the eye and the ear. However, as far as seeing and hearing are concerned, a far greater truth lies beyond all this.

To Whom Does the Consciousness That Sees and Hears within the Brain Belong?

Who watches an alluring world in the brain, listens to symphonies and the twittering of birds, and smells the rose?

The stimulations coming from a person's eyes, ears, and nose travel to the brain as electro-chemical nerve impulses. In biology, physiology, and biochemistry books, you can find many details about how this image forms in the brain. However, you will never come across the most important fact: Who perceives these electro-chemical nerve impulses as images, sounds, odors, and sensory events in the brain? There is a consciousness in the brain that perceives all this without feeling any need for an eye, an ear, and a nose. To whom does this consciousness belong? Of course it does not belong to the nerves, the fat layer, and neurons comprising the brain. This is why Darwinist-materialists, who believe that everything is comprised of matter, cannot answer these questions.

For this consciousness is the spirit created by Allah, which needs neither the eye to watch the images nor the ear to hear the sounds. Furthermore, it does not need the brain to think.

Everyone who reads this explicit and scientific fact should ponder on Almighty Allah, and fear and seek refuge in Him, for He squeezes the entire universe in a pitch-dark place of a few cubic centimeters in a three-dimensional, colored, shadowy, and luminous form.

A Materialist Faith

The information we have presented so far shows us that the theory of evolution is a incompatible with scientific findings. The theory's claim regarding the origin of life is inconsistent with science, the evolutionary mechanisms it proposes have no evolutionary power, and fossils demonstrate that the required intermediate forms have never existed. So, it certainly follows that the theory of evolution should be pushed aside as an unscientific idea. This is how many ideas, such as the Earth-centered universe model, have been taken out of the agenda of science throughout history.

However, the theory of evolution is kept on the agenda of science. Some people even try to represent criticisms directed against it as an "attack on science." Why?

The reason is that this theory is an indispensable dogmatic belief for some circles. These circles are blindly devoted to materialist philosophy and adopt Darwinism because it is the only materialist explanation that can be put forward to explain the workings of nature.

Interestingly enough, they also confess this fact from time to time. A well-known geneticist and an outspoken evolutionist, Richard C. Lewontin from Harvard University, confesses that he is "first and foremost a materialist and then a scientist":

It is not that the methods and institutions of science somehow compel us accept a material explanation of the phenomenal world, but, on the contrary, that we are forced by our a priori adherence to material causes to create an apparatus of investigation and a set of concepts that produce material explanations, no matter how counter-intuitive, no matter how mystifying to the uninitiated. Moreover, that materialism is absolute, so we cannot allow a Divine Foot in the door.[19]

These are explicit statements that Darwinism is a dogma kept alive just for the sake of adherence to materialism. This dogma maintains that there is no being save matter. Therefore, it argues that inanimate, unconscious matter created life. It insists that millions of different living species (e.g., birds, fish, giraffes, tigers, insects, trees, flowers, whales, and human beings) originated as a result of the interactions between matter such as pouring rain, lightning flashes, and so on, out of inanimate matter. This is a precept contrary both to reason and science. Yet Darwinists continue to defend it just so as "not to allow a Divine Foot in the door."

Anyone who does not look at the origin of living beings with a materialist prejudice will see this evident truth: All living beings are works of a Creator, Who is All-Powerful, All-Wise, and All-Knowing. This Creator is Allah, Who created the whole universe from non-existence, designed it in the most perfect form, and fashioned all living beings.

The Theory of Evolution is the Most Potent Spell in the World

Anyone free of prejudice and the influence of any particular ideology, who uses only his or her reason and logic, will clearly understand that belief in the theory of evolution, which brings to mind the superstitions of societies with no knowledge of science or civilization, is quite impossible.

As explained above, those who believe in the theory of evolution think that a few atoms and molecules thrown into a huge vat could produce thinking, reasoning professors and university students; such scientists as Einstein and Galileo; such artists as Humphrey Bogart, Frank Sinatra and Luciano Pavarotti; as well as antelopes, lemon trees, and carnations. Moreover, as the scientists and professors who believe in this nonsense are educated people, it is quite justifiable to speak of this theory as "the most potent spell in history." Never before has any other belief or idea so taken away peoples' powers of reason, refused to allow them to think intelligently and logically and hidden the truth from them as if they had been blindfolded. This is an even worse and unbelievable blindness than the Egyptians worshipping the Sun God Ra, totem worship in some parts of Africa, the people of Saba worshipping the Sun, the tribe of Prophet Ibrahim (peace be upon him) worshipping idols they had made with their own hands, or the people of the Prophet Musa (peace be upon him) worshipping the Golden Calf.

In fact, Allah has pointed to this lack of reason in the Qur'an. In many verse, He reveals in many verses that some peoples' minds will be closed and that they will be powerless to see the truth. Some of these verses are as follows:

As for those who do not believe, it makes no difference to them whether you warn them or do not warn them, they will not

believe. Allah has sealed up their hearts and hearing and over their eyes is a blindfold. They will have a terrible punishment. (Surat al-Baqara: 6-7)

... They have hearts with which they do not understand. They have eyes with which they do not see. They have ears with which they do not hear. Such people are like cattle. No, they are even further astray! They are the unaware. (Surat al-A'raf: 179)

Even if We opened up to them a door into heaven, and they spent the day ascending through it, they would only say: "Our eyesight is befuddled! Or rather we have been put under a spell!" (Surat al-Hijr: 14-15)

Words cannot express just how astonishing it is that this spell should hold such a wide community in thrall, keep people from the truth, and not be broken for 150 years. It is understandable that one or a few people might believe in impossible scenarios and claims full of stupidity and illogicality. However, "magic" is the only possible explanation for people from all over the world believing that unconscious and lifeless atoms suddenly decided to come together and form a universe that functions with a flawless system of organization, discipline, reason, and consciousness; a planet named Earth with all of its features so perfectly suited to life; and living things full of countless complex systems.

In fact, the Qur'an relates the incident of Prophet Musa and Pharaoh to show that some people who support atheistic philosophies actually influence others by magic. When Pharaoh was told about the true religion, he told Prophet Musa to meet with his own magicians. When Musa did so, he told them to demonstrate their abilities first. The verses continue:

He said: "You throw." And when they threw, they cast a spell on the people's eyes and caused them to feel great fear of them. They

produced an extremely powerful magic. (Surat al-A'raf: 116)

As we have seen, Pharaoh's magicians were able to deceive everyone, apart from Musa and those who believed in him. However, his evidence broke the spell, or "swallowed up what they had forged," as the verse puts it.

We revealed to Musa, "Throw down your staff." And it immediately swallowed up what they had forged. So the Truth took place and what they did was shown to be false. (Surat al-A'raf: 117-119)

As we can see, when people realized that a spell had been cast upon them and that what they saw was just an illusion, Pharaoh's magicians lost all credibility. In the present day too, unless those who, under the influence of a similar spell, believe in these ridiculous claims under their scientific disguise and spend their lives defending them, abandon their superstitious beliefs, they also will be humiliated when the full truth emerges and the spell is broken. In fact, Malcolm Muggeridge, an atheist philosopher and supporter of evolution, admitted he was worried by just that prospect:

> I myself am convinced that the theory of evolution, especially the extent to which it's been applied, will be one of the great jokes in the history books in the future. Posterity will marvel that so very flimsy and dubious an hypothesis could be accepted with the incredible credulity that it has.[20]

That future is not far off: On the contrary, people will soon see that "chance" is not a deity, and will look back on the theory of evolution as the worst deceit and the most terrible spell in the world. That spell is already rapidly beginning to be lifted from the shoulders of people all over the world. Many people who see its true face are wondering with amazement how they could ever have been taken in by it.

NOTES

1. Sidney Fox, Klaus Dose, *Molecular Evolution and The Origin of Life*, W.H. Freeman and Company, San Francisco, 1972, p. 4.

2. Alexander I. Oparin, *Origin of Life*, Dover Publications, NewYork, 1936, 1953 (reprint), p. 196.

3. "New Evidence on Evolution of Early Atmosphere and Life", *Bulletin of the American Meteorological Society*, vol 63, November 1982, p. 1328-1330.

4. Stanley Miller, *Molecular Evolution of Life: Current Status of the Prebiotic Synthesis of Small Molecules*, 1986, p. 7.

5. Jeffrey Bada, *Earth*, February 1998, p. 40

6. Leslie E. Orgel, "The Origin of Life on Earth", *Scientific American*, vol. 271, October 1994, p. 78.

7. Charles Darwin, *The Origin of Species by Means of Natural Selection*, The Modern Library, New York, p. 127.

8. Charles Darwin, *The Origin of Species: A Facsimile of the First Edition*, Harvard University Press, 1964, p. 184.

9. B. G. Ranganathan, *Origins?*, Pennsylvania: The Banner Of Truth Trust, 1988, p. 7.

10. Charles Darwin, *The Origin of Species*: *A Facsimile of the First Edition*, Harvard University Press, 1964, p. 179.

11. Derek A. Ager, "The Nature of the Fossil Record", *Proceedings of the British Geological Association*, vol 87, 1976, p. 133.

12. Douglas J. Futuyma, *Science on Trial*, Pantheon Books, New York, 1983. p. 197.

13. Solly Zuckerman, *Beyond The Ivory Tower*, Toplinger Publications, New York, 1970, pp. 75-94; Charles E. Oxnard, "The Place of Australopithecines in Human Evolution: Grounds for Doubt", Nature, vol 258, p. 389.

14. "Could science be brought to an end by scientists' belief that they have final answers or by society's reluctance to pay the bills?" *Scientific American*, December 1992, p. 20.

15. Alan Walker, *Science*, vol. 207, 7 March 1980, p. 1103; A. J. Kelso, *Physical Antropology*, 1st ed., J. B. Lipincott Co., New York, 1970, p. 221; M. D. Leakey, *Olduvai Gorge*, vol. 3, Cambridge University Press, Cambridge, 1971, p. 272.

16. Jeffrey Kluger, "Not So Extinct After All: The Primitive Homo Erectus May Have Survived Long Enough To Coexist With Modern Humans," *Time*, 23 December 1996.

17. S. J. Gould, *Natural History*, vol. 85, 1976, p. 30.

18. Solly Zuckerman, *Beyond The Ivory Tower*, p. 19.

19. Richard Lewontin, "The Demon-Haunted World," *The New York Review of Books*, January 9, 1997, p. 28.

20. Malcolm Muggeridge, *The End of Christendom*, Grand Rapids: Eerdmans, 1980, p. 43.

> They said: "Glory be to You! We have no knowledge except what You have taught us. You are the All-Knowing, the All-Wise".
> (Surat al-Baqara, 32)

Goodword English Publications

The Holy Quran: Text, Translation and Commentary (HB), Tr. Abdullah Yusuf Ali

The Holy Quran (PB), Tr. Abdullah Yusuf Ali

The Holy Quran (Laminated Board), Tr. Abdullah Yusuf Ali

The Holy Quran (HB), Tr. Abdullah Yusuf Ali

Holy Quran (Small Size), Tr. Abdullah Yusuf Ali

The Quran, Tr. T.B. Irving

The Koran, Tr. M.H. Shakir

The Glorious Quran, Tr. M.M. Pickthall

Allah is Known Through Reason, Harun Yahya

The Basic Concepts in the Quran, Harun Yahya

Crude Understanding of Disbelief, Harun Yahya

Darwinism Refuted, Harun Yahya

Death Resurrection Hell, Harun Yahya

Devoted to Allah, Harun Yahya

Eternity Has Already Begun, Harun Yahya

Ever Thought About the Truth?, Harun Yahya

The Mercy of Believers, Harun Yahya

The Miracle in the Ant, Harun Yahya

The Miracle in the Immune System, Harun Yahya

The Miracle of Man's Creation, Harun Yahya

The Miracle of Hormones, Harun Yahya

The Miracle in the Spider, Harun Yahya

The Miracle of Creation in DNA, Harun Yahya

The Miracle of Creation in Plants, Harun Yahya

The Moral Values of the Quran, Harun Yahya

The Nightmare of Disbelief, Harun Yahya

Perfected Faith, Harun Yahya

Quick Grasp of Faith, Harun Yahya

Timelessness and the Reality of Fate, Harun Yahya

In Search of God, Maulana Wahiduddin Khan

Islam and Peace, Maulana Wahiduddin Khan

An Islamic Treasury of Virtues, Maulana Wahiduddin Khan

The Moral Vision, Maulana Wahiduddin Khan

Muhammad: A Prophet for All Humanity, Maulana Wahiduddin Khan

Principles of Islam, Maulana Wahiduddin Khan

Prophet Muhammad: A Simple Guide to His Life, Maulana Wahiduddin Khan

The Quran for All Humanity, Maulana Wahiduddin Khan

The Quran: An Abiding Wonder, Maulana Wahiduddin Khan

Religion and Science, Maulana Wahiduddin Khan

Simple Wisdom (HB), Maulana Wahiduddin Khan

Simple Wisdom (PB), Maulana Wahiduddin Khan

The True Jihad, Maulana Wahiduddin Khan

Tabligh Movement, Maulana Wahiduddin Khan

A Treasury of the Quran, Maulana Wahiduddin Khan

Woman Between Islam and Western Society, Maulana Wahiduddin Khan

Woman in Islamic Shari'ah, Maulana Wahiduddin Khan

The Ideology of Peace, Maulana Wahiduddin Khan

Indian Muslims, Maulana Wahiduddin Khan

Introducing Islam, Maulana Wahiduddin Khan

Islam: Creator of the Modern Age, Maulana Wahiduddin Khan

Islam: The Voice of Human Nature, Maulana Wahiduddin Khan

Islam Rediscovered, Maulana Wahiduddin Khan

Words of the Prophet Muhammad, Maulana Wahiduddin Khan

God Arises, Maulana Wahiduddin Khan

The Call of the Qur'an, Maulana Wahiduddin Khan

Building a Strong and Prosperous India and Role of Muslims, Maulana Wahiduddin Khan

Islam As It Is, Maulana Wahiduddin Khan

Sermons of the Prophet Muhammad, Assad Nimer Busool